Chinese, Japanese, and Korean Inroads into Central Asia

Comparative Analysis of the Economic Cooperation Roadmaps for Uzbekistan

About the East-West Center

The East-West Center promotes better relations and understanding among the people and nations of the United States, Asia, and the Pacific through cooperative study, research, and dialogue. Established by the US Congress in 1960, the Center serves as a resource for information and analysis on critical issues of common concern, bringing people together to exchange views, build expertise, and develop policy options.

The Center's 21-acre Honolulu campus, adjacent to the University of Hawai'i at Mānoa, is located midway between Asia and the US mainland and features research, residential, and international conference facilities. The Center's Washington, DC, office focuses on preparing the United States for an era of growing Asia Pacific prominence.

The Center is an independent, public, nonprofit organization with funding from the US government, and additional support provided by private agencies, individuals, foundations, corporations, and governments in the region.

Policy Studies
an East-West Center series

Description

Policy Studies presents original research on pressing economic and political policy challenges for governments and industry across Asia, and for the region's relations with the United States. Written for the policy and business communities, academics, journalists, and the informed public, the peer-reviewed publications in this series provide new policy insights and perspectives based on extensive fieldwork and rigorous scholarship.

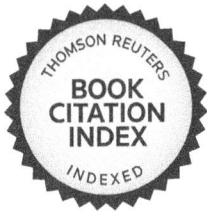

Policy Studies is indexed in the Web of Science Book Citation Index. The Web of Science is the largest and most comprehensive citation index available.

Notes to Contributors

Submissions may take the form of a proposal or complete manuscript. For more information on the Policy Studies series, please contact the Series Editors.

Editors, Policy Studies
East-West Center
1601 East-West Road
Honolulu, Hawai'i 96848-1601
Tel: 808.944.7197
Publications@EastWestCenter.org
EastWestCenter.org/PolicyStudies

Policy
Studies | 78

Chinese, Japanese, and Korean Inroads into Central Asia

Comparative Analysis of the Economic Cooperation Roadmaps for Uzbekistan

Timur Dadabaev

Chinese, Japanese, and Korean Inroads into Central Asia: Comparative Analysis of the Economic Cooperation Roadmaps for Uzbekistan
Timur Dadabaev

ISSN 1547-1349 (print) and 1547-1330 (electronic)
ISBN 978-0-86638-285-4 (print) and 978-0-86638-284-7 (electronic)

Print copies are available from Amazon.com. Free electronic copies of most titles are available on the East-West Center website, at EastWestCenter.org/PolicyStudies, where submission guidelines can also be found. Questions about the series should be directed to:

Publications Office
East-West Center
1601 East-West Road
Honolulu, Hawai'i 96848-1601

Telephone: 808.944.7197

EWCBooks@EastWestCenter.org
EastWestCenter.org/PolicyStudies

Contents

List of Acronyms

BRI   Belt and Road Initiative

CA   Central Asia

CASIC   Chinese Aerospace Science and Industry Corporation

IGC   Intergovernmental Committee

IR   International Relations

KNOC   Korea National Corporation

KEPCO   Korea Electric Power Corporation

KOICA   Korea International Cooperation Agency

KTNET   Korea Trade Network

KIRAM   Korean Institute of Rare Metals

KRICT   Korean Research Institute of Chemical Technology

MOFA   Ministry of Foreign Affairs

ODA	Official Development Assistance
ROTOBO	Japan Association for Trade with Russia & NIS
SCO	Shanghai Cooperation Organization
WTO	World Trade Organization

List of Figures

Chinese, Japanese, and Korean Inroads into Central Asia
Comparative Analysis of the Economic Cooperation Roadmaps for Uzbekistan

Placing China, Japan, and Korea in Central Asia

Many studies have been published in recent years focusing on the foreign policy of various powers in Asia. These studies tend to focus primarily on the countries and areas in Asia that have historically received extensive attention, particularly China, Japan, and South Korea in East Asia. However, few studies go beyond traditionally covered areas to focus on parts of Asia that, while becoming central to various international engagements, remain overlooked. One such example of an area not paid due attention in the literature on comparative aspects of the foreign engagements of Japan, China, and Korea is what can be referred as the last "new frontier" in Asia—Central Asia (CA) (Dadabaev 2018b).

The post-Soviet CA region—consisting of the five stans of Uzbekistan, Kazakhstan, Kyrgyzstan, Tajikistan, and Turkmenistan—has remained marginal for Asian scholars for a number of reasons. First, this region has often been associated with the geopolitically determined larger Eurasian region consisting of Russia and other post-Soviet constituents. Thus, for many scholars in International Relations (IR), this region has been approached through the analysis of Russian and post-Soviet policies, while the Asian angle of CA states' interactions has been overshadowed and to some extent hijacked by Russia-related scholarship.[1] Second, those few studies that paid attention to the CA states' interactions with Asian powerhouses, in comparative perspective, tended to focus on these states' participation in the Shanghai Cooperation Organization (SCO) or their foreign policies related to the recently announced Belt and Road Initiative (BRI).[2] Thus, once again, the framing of the CA region's coverage within the Asian political space has been hijacked by the attention paid to China-related initiatives, often with the rise of China and its global and regional economic influence as underpinning.[3] Third, those studies that intended to cover CA states' engagements with Asian countries frequently focused on individual case studies of CA-China, CA-Japan, or engagements between this region and South Korea.[4] Very few studies, if any, have attempted to consider the mutual importance of CA states and powerful Asian countries in such interactions.[5] In addition, differences and similarities in Chinese, Japanese, and Korean interactions have rarely been compared.[6] However, any conclusions on the role and significance of the Asian vector in foreign policies for CA states are difficult to make without an empirically grounded comparison of CA interactions with the most important and active states in this region: China, Japan, and South Korea.

China, Japan, and South Korea have been actively involved in various developments in CA since CA states' independence from the Soviet Union in 1991

China, Japan, and South Korea have been actively involved in various developments in CA since CA states' independence from the Soviet Union in 1991. In 1996, China launched its confidence-building mechanism, which became the Shanghai Five (three CA states, Russia, and China) and later, in 2000, the SCO.[7] These efforts resulted in significant progress in confidence-building, the resolution of border-related issues between these states, and the construction of a mechanism for combating terrorism, extremism, and separatism in this region. Almost a decade later, China launched a new "Silk Road offensive" aimed at enhancing economic cooperation among the countries of the ancient Silk Road, which was partly a response to the stalled SCO. This initiative also represented a Chinese response to alternative ideas for economic cooperation in Eurasia, namely, the Eurasian Economic Union.[8]

Japanese involvement in this region was also especially significant in supporting the early nationhood of CA states in the early 1990s. This support was framed within the Eurasian (Silk Road) Diplomacy championed by Prime Minister Ryutaro Hashimoto in 1997.[9] It was subsequently supported by prime ministers Keizo Obuchi, Yoshiro Mori, and Junichiro Koizumi. By the early 2000s, Japan became one of the largest, if not the largest, Official Development Assistance (ODA) providers to the CA countries. Such ODA support has been translated into a region-building initiative by Japan. In particular, the Japanese government initiated the establishment of a Central Asia plus Japan dialogue in 2004, which aimed not only to establish a communications channel be-

Japan became one of the largest, if not the largest, Official Development Assistance (ODA) providers to the CA countries

tween Japan and CA states but also, and importantly, to encourage discussions of various regional problems by regional states. In this sense, the Japanese initiative has been one of the most significant decolonizing initiatives (offering alternatives to Russian and possibly Chinese funding and infrastructure, which were formerly routed through Russia) undertaken by non-regional powers in CA because it offered not only a forum for such discussions but also practical financial support from Japan toward projects on which more than two CA countries can reach a mutually acceptable agreement.[10] To emphasize the importance of CA to Japan, then Japanese Prime Minister Koizumi visited Uzbekistan and Kazakhstan in 2006. A decade later, in October of 2015, Prime Minister Shinzo Abe visited all five CA republics, promoting new initiatives such as high-quality infrastructure[11] and the Free and Open Indo-Pacific Strategy to further advance Japanese corporate interests internationally and in the CA region.[12] Japan has displayed significant commitment toward the region, demonstrated by the scale of its support toward CA states as indicated in Table 1.[13]

Table 1. Japanese ODA Offered to the Countries of Central Asia on a Bilateral Basis by Country (USD million)

	2001	2002	2003	2004	2005	2006
Uzbekistan	30.92	40.16	63.22	99.75	60.02	29.60
Kazakhstan	43.93	30.13	136.27	134.34	69.68	28.19
Kyrgyz Rep	23.15	8.12	31.23	26.69	20.95	17.22
Tajikistan	4.61	26.96	4.77	6.58	9.93	8.04
Turkmenistan	16.42	11.37	6.80	2.22	0.13	0.62

	2007	2008	2009	2010	2011	2012	2013
Uzbekistan	70.29	64.53	41.92	34.08	31.26	26.25	56.49
Kazakhstan	55.39	56.63	63.38	30.56	19.79	30.89	36.99
Kyrgyz Rep	15.69	12.49	18.06	23.50	30.99	19.98	17.87
Tajikistan	9.43	8.06	26.24	43.42	35.59	32.98	26.66
Turkmenistan	0.38	0.57	1.15	1.55	1.27	0.53	0.56

Source: Compiled from the data made available by the Ministry of Foreign Affairs of Japan, *Seifu Kaihatsu Enjyo (ODA) Kunibetsu de-tabuku 2014* (*Chuou ajia/kokasasu chiiki*), [Official Development Assistance by Country Data Book 2014 (Region of Central Asia and Caucasus)], Tokyo, Japan, accessed July 15, 2015, http://www.mofa.go.jp/mofaj/gaiko/oda/files/000072593.pdf.

The South Korean presence in both CA and Uzbekistan, in particular, demonstrates some additional features in addition to those seen in the Chinese and the Japanese policies. Similar to Japan in the two cases described above, South Korea has demonstrated a desire for its own region-building scheme along the lines of Korea plus Central Asia, which to some extent was influenced by learning about the experiences of the Central Asia plus Japan initiative. However, some features distinguish Korea from China and Japan. The first is the presence of the large Korean diaspora, whose influence on foreign policy has been overstated by previous studies merely because its majority can be referred to as Korean only to a relative degree. Many, if not all, of the Korean diaspora speak Russian as their primary language, while those who speak Korean had to learn it as a foreign language. Their degree of association with the aims and goals of Korean foreign policy in CA is uncertain simply because Korean foreign policy in the region is very diverse and does not include the idea of uniting all those who are referred to as part of the Korean diaspora. To some extent, though, the presence of a Korean diaspora can also be related to increased people-to-people contacts and Korean visa policy, which is discussed in the second half of this paper. The second feature manifest in the Korean penetration of CA is the fact that Korean private/corporate interests are visibly more active and flexible when compared to public institutions and governmental agencies. By the time the Korean government properly framed its initiative, roughly 15 years after the collapse of the USSR, South Korean Daewoo, Samsung, LG, Daewoo Unitel (a communications company), Kabool Textiles (a cotton processing and textile production company), and many other brands had thriving businesses in car manufacturing, textile processing, and electronics assembly, most notably in Uzbekistan and Kazakhstan. Thus, the successes of these enterprises have pulled the Korean government's larger involvement into CA in a spillover effect. Essentially, the successes of individual Korean enterprises sent a message to the Korean government that CA, and Uzbekistan, in particular, is an area where Korean (public and corporate) interests have great potential. This process has led to the Joint Declaration on Strategic Partnership with Uzbekistan in 2006 as well as other agreements opening new frontiers, including extraction agreements with the Korea National Oil Corporation (KNOC) in 2006; Uzbekneftegaz's granting to KNOC exclusive exploration rights to the Chust-Pap, Namangan-Terachi, the Surgil gas fields in 2008; and purchases of uranium by the Korea Electric Power Corporation (KEPCO) in 2008, to name a few. Navoi airport has become another infrastructure project, with the Hanjin Group establishing and developing a Navoi logistical hub with a certain degree of success.

Thus, by the time South Korea's Silk Road diplomacy was announced in 2009, South Korea's economic presence in CA, particularly in Kazakhstan and Uzbekistan, was significant in terms of ODA assistance (drawn by corporate successes of the early 1990s and 2000s), direct investments, and human resource development. The Korea International Cooperation Agency (KOICA) has been allocating significant funds for various human-resource development projects that were considered not only to be contributing to Uzbekistan but also to be preparing human resources needed for the Korean presence in CA and for South Koreans domestically. President Lee Myung-bak again visited CA in 2011 and took part in the opening of several enterprises with South Korean capital. This visit was followed by the initiation of a South Korea plus Central Asia dialogue. In this sense, in contrast with China and Japan, Korean region-building did not start from political initiatives but instead grew out of economic and social engagement with the region.

The third feature that distinguishes Korea's engagement from that of China and Japan is the aspect of people-to-people communication. Here again, one can distinguish among these three cases. In the case of China, the access of the CA population to China is extremely limited, with visas very difficult to obtain, despite all the rhetoric of friendship between China and CA states. This limitation again shows that China is not interested in promoting people-to-people communications because it sees more threats than benefits from such contacts (namely, support for repressed ethnic Turkic groups such as Uighurs within China). Japan maintains a fair amount of people-to-people contacts with many scholarships extended to CA students and, in recent years, has eased visa regimes to allow those satisfying certain criteria to visit Japan for social reasons. Uzbekistan, along with other CA republics, has abolished a visa requirement for short-term visits for Japanese tourists. In addition, South Korea is perhaps the most advanced in these policies, as it not only issues visitation permits and visas for Uzbeks but also, importantly, attracts abundant human resources into the Korean labor market. In fact, Uzbeks (all those carrying Uzbek citizenship, including Uzbek citizenship holders of Korean descent) currently rank as the 5th largest group among foreigners residing in South Korea (at approx. 55,000 or 3% of all foreigners), following foreign residents from China (approx. 1 million residents or 50%), Vietnam (approx. 150,000 or 7.3 percent), the United States (approx. 140,000 or 6.8 percent), and Thailand (approx. 100,000 or 5 percent).[14] As this statistic shows, the level of

Uzbeks currently rank as the 5th largest group among foreigners residing in South Korea

Uzbekistan's connection with and penetration by South Korea is not limited to corporate contacts only but extends to social spheres to a degree that cannot be compared to China and Japan.

As clearly outlined above, these East Asian countries have significant influence in the CA region and are increasingly diversifying their areas of interest. China ranks the highest in trade with Uzbekistan, while Korea is among the top economic partners, as seen in Figure 1. Japan is one of the largest ODA providers to CA, and to Uzbekistan in particular.

Figure 1. Uzbekistan's Main Trading Partners and Trade Volumes, 2017 (percent of total)

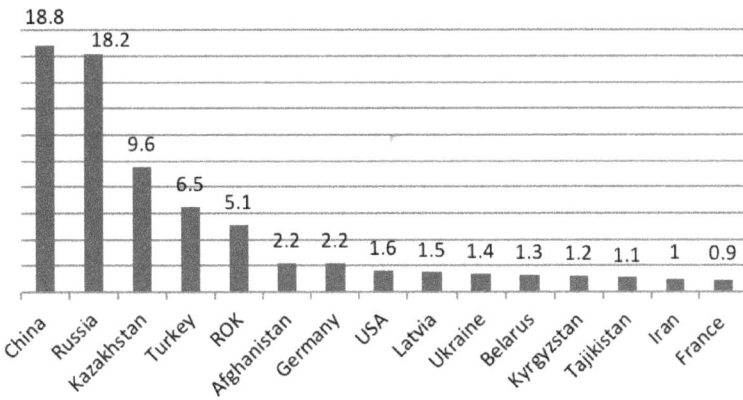

Source: Vneshne-torgovyi balans Uzbekistana sostavil 17.8 milliarda [External Trade Balance of Uzbekistan Reached USD 17.8 billion], Gazeta, August 14, 2018, accessed August 14, 2018, https://www.gazeta.uz/ru/2018/08/13/foreign-trade/.

Despite the significant influence these states have, little if any literature focuses on the nuances of their influences and the features of their involvement rather than solely on the perceived rivalry among them. In addition, few details of their projects are provided, with no attempt to evaluate their performance in the CA region from a comparative perspective.

To fill this gap, this study aims to shed light on the place and role of CA states and Asian powerhouses (such as China, Japan, and Korea) in one another's policies. To do so, this study analyzes the economic cooperation roadmaps agreed upon between governments of CA states and China, Japan, and South Korea in 2017. Because coverage of all CA states is logistically difficult within this study, Uzbekistan has been selected as the case for CA states, and the cooperation roadmaps between Uzbekistan and its East Asian counterparts are this paper's main analytical focus.

This paper raises the following research questions. What are the areas of interest for China, Japan, and Korea in their relations with CA states? What are the patterns of agenda-setting in establishing intergovernmental cooperation? What are the particular projects that these states initiate? What are the objectives of projects initiated within these areas of interest? How competitive or complementary are these projects of China, Japan, and Korea?

Structurally, this study consists of five main sections. The first section details the reasons for choosing cooperation roadmaps in analyzing intergovernmental cooperation. This section also outlines the reasons for focusing on Uzbekistan among other CA states while indicating the significance of this analysis for understanding Chinese, Japanese, and Korean foreign policies. The second section then analyzes the patterns of agenda-setting, the actors in such processes, and the process of constructing cooperation roadmaps between China, Japan, and Korea and their CA counterparts, as exemplified by Uzbekistan. The third, fourth, and fifth sections then discuss country specificities of Chinese, Japanese, and Korean roadmaps with Uzbekistan and highlight their similarities and differences. The final section compares the similarities and differences among these states in their cooperation schemes with CA states.

Why Is It All About the Roadmaps?

The analysis of the economic cooperation roadmaps—sets of step-by-step plans for cooperation—is chosen as this paper's main methodological tool for two reasons. First, while discourses on the intentions of various powers in engaging CA states have been analyzed on multiple occasions, few studies, if any, consider the particular projects these states plan and analyze their reasoning and implementation. Second, while speeches and statements of presidents, foreign ministers, and policy officials inform our understanding of the relations between CA and East Asian states, the roadmaps of cooperation demonstrate how these politically articulated intentions materialize in the practical realm. That is not to say that roadmaps are necessarily realizable plans. However, they are the most tangible plans that are closest to the practical outcomes of governments' articulated intentions and discourses. In this sense, this study attempts to understand the practical nuances of the engagement of China, Japan, and Korea in this region by analyzing plan outlines within roadmaps worked out by intergovernmental committees (IGC) of related states.

In terms of country coverage, ideally outlines of roadmaps of all CA states in their relations with China, Japan, and Korea would be analyzed. However, this task is logistically difficult as analyzing all roadmaps would require a significantly larger study that would need not only to analyze the roadmaps between CA and East Asian countries but also to compare various roadmaps between CA states. Therefore, this paper focuses on the analysis of the Chinese, Japanese, and Korean cooperation roadmaps with Uzbekistan.

There are also multiple reasons for choosing Uzbekistan. First, Uzbekistan is the largest CA state in terms of population. Uzbekistan's stability and development impact the sustainability of CA regional development. Second, Uzbekistan is one of the few CA states that attempt to build an equal balance in its relations with Russia, the EU, and Asian states, which it does by always emphasizing that China, Japan, and Korea are strategically important partners. In comparison to Uzbekistan, other CA states, such as Kazakhstan, Kyrgyzstan, or Tajikistan, tend to be over-dependent on Russia (through membership in the Eurasian Economic Community and Eurasian Economic Union) or on China (through a huge share of debt). In contrast, Uzbekistan pursued a foreign policy aimed at limiting its dependence on international actors by eschewing military alliances and balancing relations with larger powers. In this sense, Uzbekistan is uniquely positioned for analysis as the country that, while not necessarily favoring one of

> *Uzbekistan always emphasizes that China, Japan, and Korea are strategically important partners*

these states as its most important economic partner, still attempts to define the importance of each of these states for its economy. Third, Uzbekistan is the state that is currently transitioning from the previous president Islam Karimov's dictatorial type of government to openness, embracing foreign engagements with various countries in the post-Karimov era.[15] Thus, the case of Uzbekistan demonstrates the challenges of CA states in their engagements with their more powerful Asian counterparts. In addition, an analysis of Uzbekistan's post-Karimov era economic engagements with East Asian countries demonstrates the elements of continuity and change in its foreign policy, thereby offering insights into the country's behavior for the foreseeable future. Finally, the choice of Uzbekistan is unique from the perspective of inquiry into the foreign policy of China, Japan, and Korea. None of these states enjoyed necessarily friendly relations with CA in general or with Uzbekistan in particular prior to the collapse of the Soviet Union, because these states were constituents of the Soviet sphere. Since the collapse of the Soviet Union, these countries have represented the new political and economic frontier where China, Japan, and Korea can construct their relations in the conditions of a changing international order and the changing nature of their international standings. All of these states launched their initiatives in Uzbekistan in 1991. Thus, their starting positions in these regions were somewhat similar. Having now grown into the second-largest world economy, China is adapting to the necessity of dealing with smaller neighbors such as Uzbekistan. Japan and Korea are also in the process of adapting their behavior to the conditions in which their economic power has faded compared to China while seeing the need to expand their outreach into the CA region in search for new opportunities. Japan is in search of a new place and role in this Japan-friendly region where there is an articulate expectation of a larger Japanese presence, as demonstrated by various polls. Korea has invested heavily through its corporate penetration in CA and thus is interested in expanding its economic presence. This is especially important for Korea's presence in Uzbekistan, where it enjoys support from the government after the successful visit of the Uzbek president to South Korea in 2017. In addition, both countries are engaged in region-building efforts with the Central Asia plus Japan initiative and the Korea plus Central Asia forum. While these are not counterpoised to the Chinese SCO and BRI schemes, they represent Japanese and Korean efforts to present an alternative "other" to CA states. In this sense, the analysis of roadmaps of cooperation provides insights into foreign policy behaviors and factors that are important both for efficient cooperation and for shedding light on the possible challenges in engagements with CA states, exemplified by the case of Uzbekistan with China, Japan, and Korea.

The Economic Cooperation Roadmaps and the Agenda-Setting Structure

The role of intergovernmental cooperation in designing agreements is often demonstrated in bringing to conclusion contracts among state institutions, state agencies, and various corporations, many of which depend on governmental support. However, in negotiations between countries with limited market economies or excessive state presence in their economic activities, governments play significant functions that serve to guide state and non-state enterprises to motivate these actors in economic activities in order to move toward certain directions that the government prioritizes.[16]

In the case of post-Soviet CA states, exemplified by their engagement with Uzbekistan, the government represents the developmental apparatus that frequently defines the areas of strategic importance and negotiates with foreign governments in cooperating toward those goals. To some extent, such developmental functions, inclusive of foreign policy, are also shared by the governments of China, Japan, and South Korea, making it easier for these countries to conduct their negotiations.

The government represents the developmental apparatus that frequently defines the areas of strategic importance

In terms of the negotiation structure between China, Japan, South Korea, and Uzbekistan, they normally begin by establishing each state's objectives and goals as defined in their domestic developmental goals and programs. Each of these is communicated at different levels, but most conventionally through the channels of the ministries of foreign affairs. Often, such communications intensify when approximate dates for visits of heads of state, governments, or foreign ministers are decided. Once those domestic programs and goals are mutually articulated and duly recognized, the possible areas of cooperation are distilled from those programs. Most typically for the countries covered in this paper, the areas of trade, transportation infrastructure development, energy resource exploitation, innovation, and technologies and security are considered to be of primary importance. The degree of importance of each area fluctuates depending on the country. For instance, in cooperation with China, infrastructure development and security feature prominently, while in cooperation with Japan and South Korea human development, technological innovation, and modernization of infrastructure receive higher attention and importance. Once the areas of cooperation are defined, each government involved designates the main actor responsible for promoting cooperation within this area. In the case of Uzbekistan and some other post-Soviet states, the degree of centralization of governmental functions is very significant and often results in a situation where a single ministry (for instance the ministry of economy) is the main actor in negotiating cooperation in several areas (such as infrastructure, transportation, or energy resources). In the cases of China, Japan, and South Korea, the situation drastically differs from one case to another. For instance, in the case of China the degree of centralization is somewhat close to CA states, so the same ministry is often responsible for promoting cooperation in the same area. In the cases of Japan and South Korea, the situation is very different, largely reflecting the degree of economic liberalization and the central government's decentralization, as described in the country-specific parts of this study. Once the main actors are defined by each government, these actors determine the most appropriate agencies and actors to assist them in promoting this area of cooperation.

This process prepares the stage for proposals to be forwarded by all actors within the area of cooperation to be included in the proposal for action map. Normally, each side considers proposals for each area and then decides whether they want to forward these proposals to their counterparts. Initial discussions can be held through channels provided by ministries of foreign affairs and unofficially signaled to counterparts. In certain other cases, the actors of a potential cooperation scheme visit the country or site of possible cooperation to assess both the potential and the challenges for developing a successful cooperation scheme. This action is also often needed when certain public or private enterprises design their business plans, which requires a detailed assessment of local conditions, needed investments, and possible revenues to be generated from the project. Such potential plans are preliminarily signaled to the counterpart's ministry of foreign affairs (MOFA), simplifying the process of facilitating the visits and gaining access to the data required for risk calculation. In this sense, the roles played by the governments in such cooperation schemes might not be necessarily to invest public funds into these projects but rather to provide a secure environment for private enterprises to enter the markets of countries they traditionally consider to be risk prone, such as Uzbekistan. Once the projects are offered as proposals, a meeting is held between the intergovernmental committee on cooperation and its subcommittees focusing on particular areas and consisting of representatives of both sides.

When the interests of the different sides do not match, they move on to projects that are of greater mutual interest. In this sense, the establishment of the committee and the respective subcommittees creates a channel of communication and a sort of bargaining table that is open throughout the year on an ad hoc basis. This committee and its subcommittees are also a good way to signal certain policy and priority changes for each country. They help prevent miscommunications at the political level and provide coordination capacity for enterprise activity.

Figure 2. The Structure of the Initiation of Cooperation for Uzbekistan

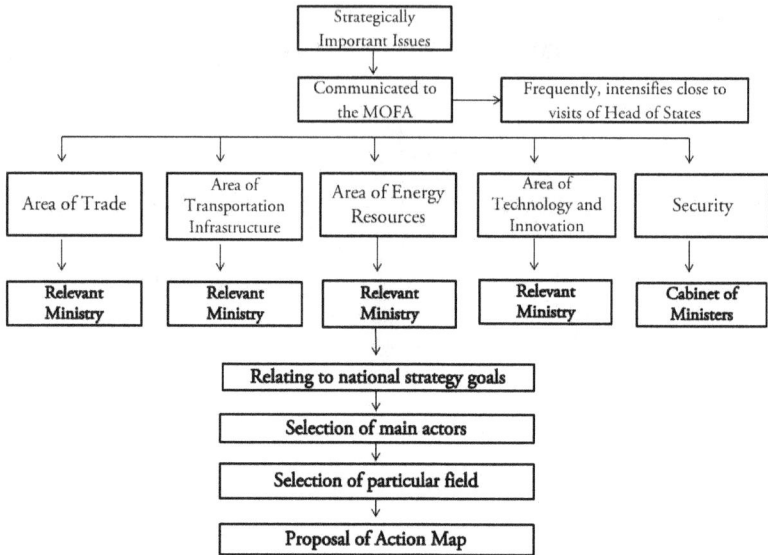

```
                      ┌─────────────────┐
                      │  Strategically  │
                      │ Important Issues│
                      └────────┬────────┘
                               ↓
              ┌──────────────────┐     ┌──────────────────────────────┐
              │ Communicated to  │ ──→ │ Frequently, intensifies close to │
              │   the MOFA       │     │   visits of Head of States      │
              └──────────────────┘     └──────────────────────────────┘
```

Area of Trade	Area of Transportation Infrastructure	Area of Energy Resources	Area of Technology and Innovation	Security
Relevant Ministry	Relevant Ministry	Relevant Ministry	Relevant Ministry	Cabinet of Ministers

Relating to national strategy goals
Selection of main actors
Selection of particular field
Proposal of Action Map

While the Chinese government is well prepared and experienced in playing such leading and often developmental roles for its corporations and enterprises, the case of Japan demonstrates that the Japanese government is rather hesitant to play an active role in facilitating private enterprise entry into the CA region, primarily because Japan has a completely liberalized and free market economy. In such a structure, Japan's government (and the Japanese MOFA in particular) is rather hesitant to play a role in singling out a particular enterprise and promoting its interests, which might be interpreted as governmental interference into economic activity. Such a situation, however, does not necessarily represent a structural problem, and there continues to be an opportunity for the Japanese government to promote its private enterprises in the CA region without being accused of interference, as detailed in the section on the Japanese roadmaps below.

The Korean case is somewhat different. Although in the Chinese and the Japanese cases the central government is frequently the engine for encouraging direct investments into CA economies, in the Korean case private enterprises are far more active in promoting cooperation, while the government plays reactive roles with respect to such entrepreneurial activities. The Korean government does not play the pivotal role in initiating entrepreneurial activities, but it is often pulled into playing a more prominent role in the region where Korean enterprises have already built a significant economic presence. In addition, the spillover effect occurs to a certain degree in Korean involvement in this region when successful projects by certain enterprises encourage development of similar ones in other areas that are predominantly private interest driven. Such a spillover effect is not necessarily observed in the cases of Chinese and Japanese private participation.[17]

Once the proposals for each of the main actors responsible for cooperation in these areas are considered and analyzed, only those deemed to potentially produce tangible short-to-mid-term outcomes are included in the proposals for each area of cooperation. The proposals are then grouped into framework agreements, contracts, and memorandums that constitute the backbone of intergovernmental cooperation roadmaps (see Figure 3). In this sense, the intergovernmental cooperation roadmaps are sets of plans, agreements, and memorandums that document commonly shared norms, approaches, and objectives between Uzbekistan on the one hand and China, Japan, or Korea on the other.

Figure 3. The Structure of Agreements

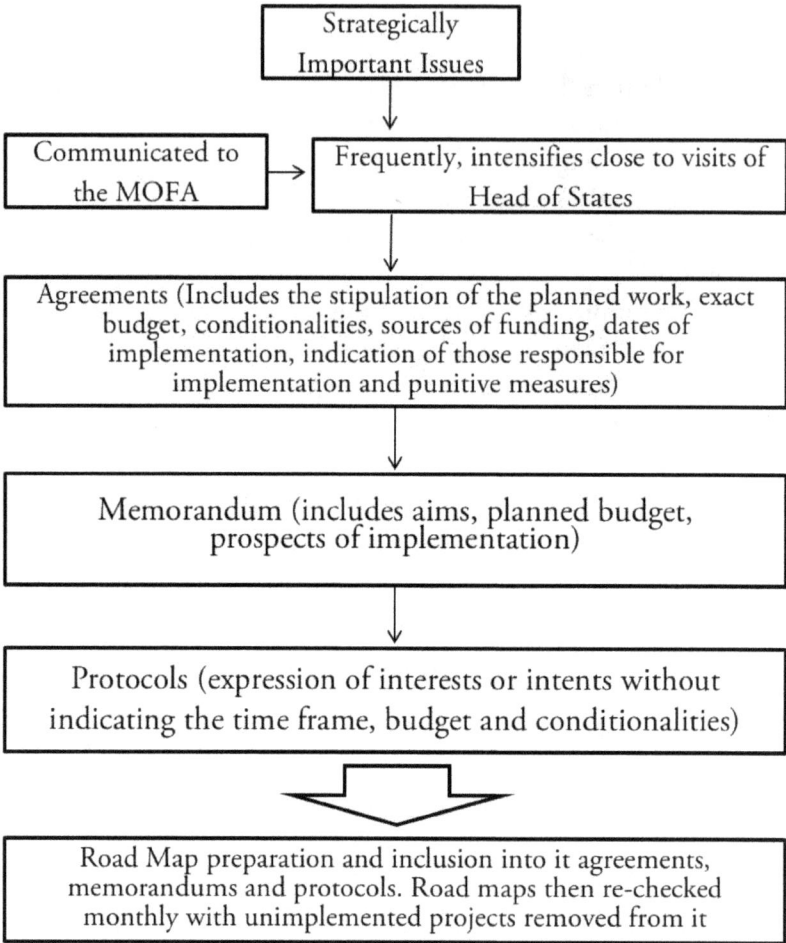

```
                    ┌─────────────────────┐
                    │    Strategically    │
                    │  Important Issues   │
                    └─────────────────────┘
                               │
                               ▼
┌──────────────────┐   ┌─────────────────────────────────────────┐
│  Communicated to │ → │ Frequently, intensifies close to visits of│
│     the MOFA     │   │            Head of States                │
└──────────────────┘   └─────────────────────────────────────────┘
                               │
                               ▼
┌─────────────────────────────────────────────────────────────────┐
│ Agreements (Includes the stipulation of the planned work, exact   │
│  budget, conditionalities, sources of funding, dates of           │
│  implementation, indication of those responsible for              │
│  implementation and punitive measures)                            │
└─────────────────────────────────────────────────────────────────┘
                               │
                               ▼
┌─────────────────────────────────────────────────────────────────┐
│     Memorandum (includes aims, planned budget,                    │
│            prospects of implementation)                           │
└─────────────────────────────────────────────────────────────────┘
                               │
                               ▼
┌─────────────────────────────────────────────────────────────────┐
│     Protocols (expression of interests or intents without         │
│  indicating the time frame, budget and conditionalities)          │
└─────────────────────────────────────────────────────────────────┘
                               ▼
┌─────────────────────────────────────────────────────────────────┐
│   Road Map preparation and inclusion into it agreements,          │
│  memorandums and protocols. Road maps then re-checked             │
│  monthly with unimplemented projects removed from it              │
└─────────────────────────────────────────────────────────────────┘
```

These economic cooperation roadmaps often reflect not only on the governments' intentions and goals but also and importantly on the negotiating governments' own developmental plans, programs, and goals. These then influence the negotiations by defining the objectives of mutual cooperation as well as the place and role of these governments in each other's development. In this sense, the statements of presidents, prime ministers, foreign ministers, and heads of individual agencies matter as articulations of intent. However, unless these are integrated into intergovernmental cooperation roadmaps they do not carry much more than symbolic weight as far as policy is concerned. Thus, analysis of roadmaps is crucial and essential in understanding the practical aspects of announced cooperation goals.

Country-Specific Agenda-Setting Patterns

The issue of agenda-setting and the manner in which the agenda is set are determinants of the negotiation outcomes between various counterparts.

China, Japan, and Korea approach negotiations with CA states in seemingly similar ways, as exemplified by the case of Uzbekistan, demonstrated in Figure 4. In particular, the channeling role of the ministries of foreign affairs and governmental apparatuses is significant for establishing cooperation between these states. However, the analysis of Chinese, Japanese, and Korean interactions with Uzbekistan demonstrate a significant degree of difference between the patterns of decision-making practiced by these three East Asian powerhouses with respect to their CA counterparts, as demonstrated by the case of Uzbekistan.

Figure 4. The Structure of and Roles Played by Various Actors

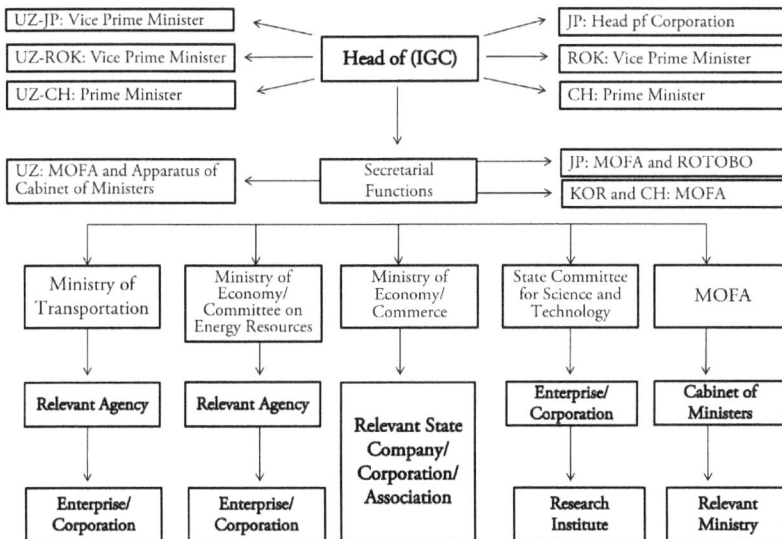

That is not to say that all of these states adhere to a completely different pattern of negotiations from one another. Interestingly, some of these countries, such as China, have a strikingly similar structure in the way the government positions itself with respect to domestic and external actors in economic interactions, as outlined below. Such a pattern of behavior on the government's part, which displays features of the developmental (as opposed to the regulatory) function, unites perspectives of the Chinese and Uzbek governments, as both seem to share an appreciation of this kind of governmental leadership. In this sense, establishing communication channels among governmental structures is detrimental to establishing effective inter-state economic ties.[18]

First, domestic signposting documents are similar and guide the agenda-setting on both the Chinese and the Uzbek sides. In the Uzbek case, this is the Development Strategy 2017–21, which has been analyzed elsewhere.[19] This document's significance is that it sets important goals and objectives for Uzbekistan's economic development, which serve as critical signposts when approaching foreign counterparts. Unless these goals and objectives are met, Uzbekistan does not display a strong desire to enter into agreements. On the Chinese side, the Ministry of Foreign Affairs, the National Development and Reform Commission, and the Ministry of Commerce drafted an action plan in 2015 outlining policy coordination, connectivity, unimpeded trade, financial cooperation, and people-to-people bonds as the primary principles of Chinese engagement in other regions, including CA (Lain 2017). The same type of commitment has been displayed by the Uzbek governmental bureaucracy, which prepared its own roadmap emphasizing cooperation at the governmental level to facilitate trade.[20]

Second, the similarities in patterns of governance between China and Uzbekistan can be cited as another factor significantly affecting cooperation's success, which for the purposes of this paper, is defined as the number of agreements signed within the framework of the economic cooperation roadmaps. In particular, in the case of China and Uzbekistan governments not only advise and assist but essentially guide their corporations into certain sectors and fields of cooperation. In such a structure, the efficiency of negotiations is greater because they involve not only governmental agencies but, importantly, the very actors in such cooperation. In countries with a completely liberal economy, like Japan or Korea, governments are limited in their ability to guide private corporations into particular fields or to select certain enterprises as primary actors of cooperation simply because governments in such liberal economies are considered to play only regulatory functions without any interference into economic activities. In this sense, the Chinese government displays a greater degree of flexibility and efficiency in attracting its enterprises to do business in CA, while for the Japanese and Korean enterprises it is a matter of taking risks and preparing local conditions for their entry into those markets.[21]

Figure 5. The Actors in and Patterns of Negotiations between China and Uzbekistan

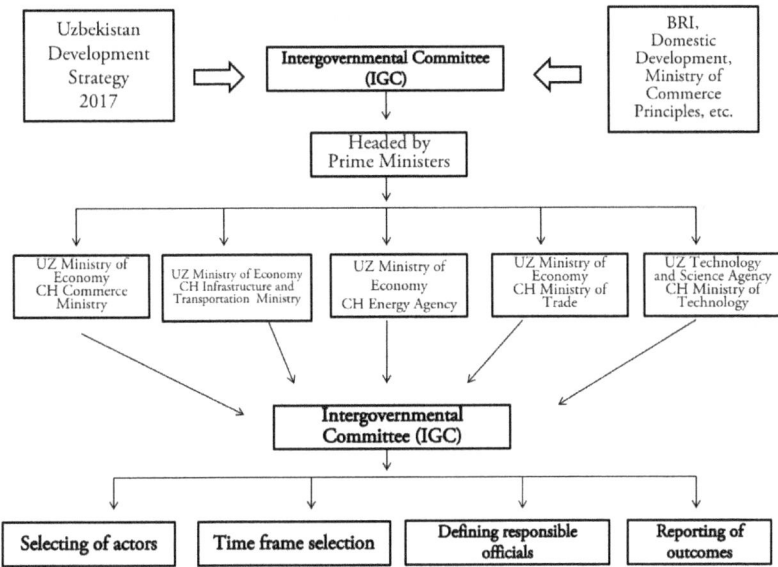

As outlined in Figure 5, negotiations are led by the Ministry of Foreign Trade, the Chamber of Commerce, and the Agency for Foreign Investments on the Uzbek side while the Cabinet of Ministers plays a coordinating function. In approaching Chinese counterparts, these actors follow the guidelines of the development strategy, seeking the best-fit partners from among potential Chinese actors to fulfill these tasks. The proposals are presented to the Uzbek-Chinese

Intergovernmental Committee for Cooperation, co-headed by the Uzbek deputy prime minister and the secretary of the Chinese Communist Party's Political-Judicial Committee (Uzbek-Chinese Intergovernmental Committee for Cooperation 2011).[22]

The intergovernmental committee's work is divided among several subcommittees, such as those on trade and economic relations (co-ordinated by the Uzbek Ministry of Foreign Trade and the Chinese Ministry of Commerce), cooperation in energy (coordinated by the Uzbek Ministry of the Economy and the PRC National Energy Administration), transportation (coordinated by the Uzbek Ministry of Foreign Trade and the PRC Ministry of Transport), technical and scientific cooperation (coordinated by the Uzbek Committee on Coordination of Science and Technology and the PRC Ministry of Science and Technology), cultural and humanitarian cooperation (coordinated by the Uzbek Ministry of Culture and the PRC Ministry of Culture), and cooperation in security-related issues (coordinated by the Uzbek Ministry of Foreign Affairs and the PRC Ministry of Foreign Affairs).[23]

These committees meet at least once a year, with the issues to be discussed communicated through the channels of the coordinating institutions well ahead of the meetings. If the needs of Uzbekistan can be met by a Chinese enterprise, the Chinese coordinating agency frequently serves as the communication line to establish the contacts and invite the potential investors from China to discuss the project. Additionally, to facilitate connections between businesses, several ministries (for instance, the Uzbek Foreign Trade Ministry and the PRC Ministry of Commerce) have signed memoranda to organize producer exhibitions, which have eventually resulted in the visit of small- and medium-sized enterprise representatives from Tianjin to the Jizzakh and Sirdarya free economic areas and the decision to al-locate certain areas in Jizzakh exclusively for entrepreneurs from that region of China.[24]

However, this coordination capacity is only made possible through a certain degree of structural similarity in the relations between the governments and businesses, because these governments still play a much greater role than they would in countries with Western lib-eral market economies. In addition, once an agreement is reached, the government of Uzbekistan still exercises significant control over the economic activities of the enterprises, which is problematic for companies from other countries but acceptable to Chinese corporations due to the similarity of governmental controls in China. On the Uzbek side, a separate committee is created to ensure the agreements created for each partner country are implemented. For instance, aside from China, the latest development in this regard was the creation by Uzbekistan of a national committee to ensure the implementation of agreements with the United States.[25] The committee's work is stipulated by roadmaps for cooperation with each country, and committee heads present reports on progress and the relevant directions of the roadmaps to the president between the 5th and the 10th of each month.

As a result of this work, the focus of the May 2017 visit of President Shavkat Mirziyoyev to China was obviously on the promotion of economic ties between the two countries based on the "Shanghai spirit" bargaining strategy.[26] Even before this visit, Uzbekistan and China enjoyed a fair level of economic cooperation, as seen in the list of investment projects underway prior to 2017 announced by the Uzbek Ministry of the Economy.[27] The visit marked the signing of one of the most ambitious packages of agreements, including 11 intergovernmental agreements, one intermunicipal agreement, and a package of economic contracts worth USD 22.8 billion.[28] It remains to be seen how many of these projects will reach their declared outcomes, and there is no comparable data to indicate the general ratio of implementation of these projects. However, as has been indicated to the author by the Uzbek government official anonymously interviewed in 2017, the fact of inclusion into the roadmap puts considerable pressure on government officials to do their utmost to ensure their implementation. Institutionally, the degree of implementation of these projects is checked at the governmental meetings held monthly, which when deemed necessary make needed corrections to ensure implementation of these plans.

Figure 6. Constituent Elements of the China-Uzbek Roadmap

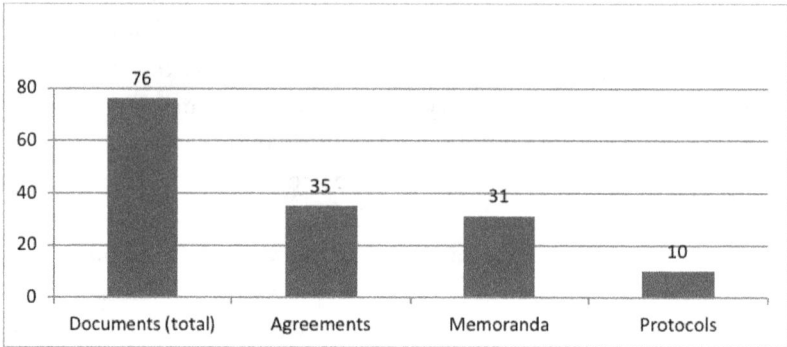

Source: "Uzbekistan i Kitai Podpisali Ryad dokumentov" [Uzbekistan and China Signed a Range of Documents], Review.uz, May 13, 2017, accessed September 23, 2017, http://www.review.uz/novosti-main/item/11214-uzbekistan-i-kitaj-podpisali-ryad-dokumentov-spisok.

As described in the sections below, the most significant areas in which Chinese roadmaps envision cooperation are manufacturing, resource-related investments, and infrastructure development.

In contrast to the Chinese agenda-setting pattern, Japan's approach represents a significantly different government-business relationship. While the Chinese-Uzbek interstate committee is primarily composed of government members, government-affiliated agencies, and state-run corporations as well as financial institutions, the Japan-Uzbek interstate cooperation committee primarily aims to unite the prospective market actors. Thus, it positions itself as an institution representing the interests of a wider spectrum of actors, going beyond governmental institutions. The main idea of governmental participation in these negotiations is that the Ministry of Foreign Affairs and other related ministries merely play the role of facilitators of the dialogue between the private economic entities and humanitarian organizations. Such a prominent role of the governments sometimes leads to the abuses of authority on the part of both the host and the investors, such as the situation when some companies (in particular Nihon Koutsu Gijyutsu [Japan Transportation Consultants][29] were caught paying bribes to Uzbek (and to Vietnamese and other states') officials in the process of ODA implementation, leading governments to place safeguards against such situations.[30]

Although the Japanese government plays an important role in arranging a proper platform for dialogue, neither the Japanese foreign ministry nor any other state body aims to adopt a developmental role (persuading the Japanese participants, assisting in selecting the companies, taking part in negotiating better treatment, etc.) or to lead the process. In addition, the Japanese government does not adopt the responsibility of defining the areas of the most pressing concern for its businesses but instead allows corporate interests to lead the discussion. In such a situation, and in Uzbekistan in particular, governmental desire alone does not represent sufficient support for certain corporate interests to get involved in CA.

As if to reflect on this difference with China, the Interstate Committee on Economic Cooperation between Japan and Uzbekistan is composed not of public officials but largely of representatives from the commercial sector. These include representatives of various corporations on the Japanese side, with the Japan Association for Trade with Russia & NIS (ROTOBO) playing the role of coordinator for these activities. This representation also demonstrates the structural mismatch between Japanese and Uzbek expectations. On the Japanese side, an expectation exists that the corporate community will express a desire to enter the Uzbek market once it gains confidence through information-sharing meetings and an increase in personal contacts. Therefore, the main actor in such interactions is the corporate community. On the Uzbek side, however, an expectation exists that the Japanese government needs to play a more active part not only in setting the stage for information exchange but more importantly in encouraging particular Japanese corporations to enter the Uzbek market. Such an expectation is well understood among Japanese policymakers. However, given the limitations of free economic enterprises, the Japanese government limits its role only to information gathering and providing basic support to its corporations. Although the Japanese government's position fits well with the principles of a liberal economic system, such a "birdwatching" stance does not seem to bring any tangible outcomes, since the other East Asian governments of China and Korea do not hesitate to openly promote the interests of particular corporations. The coordination role of ROTOBO has also been criticized both by Uzbekistan and by its Kazakh counterparts on several occasions. The reason for such criticism emanates from the fact that CA governments are represented at such meetings by representatives of ministries and state agencies that are in the position to make policy and practical decisions. At the same time, ROTOBO is an organization that is neither in a position to propose a particular policy change nor able to implement any policy decisions. It is not a part of the executive body, and most of its views and perceptions are of a consultative nature, which has little or no relevance to the policy field. In addition, the Interstate Economic Committee is mismatched: on the Japanese side, it is jointly led by the representative of a Japanese corporation while on the Uzbek side it is supervised by the prime minister or the deputy prime minister.

Figure 7. Japan-Uzbek Economic Cooperation Committee Composition

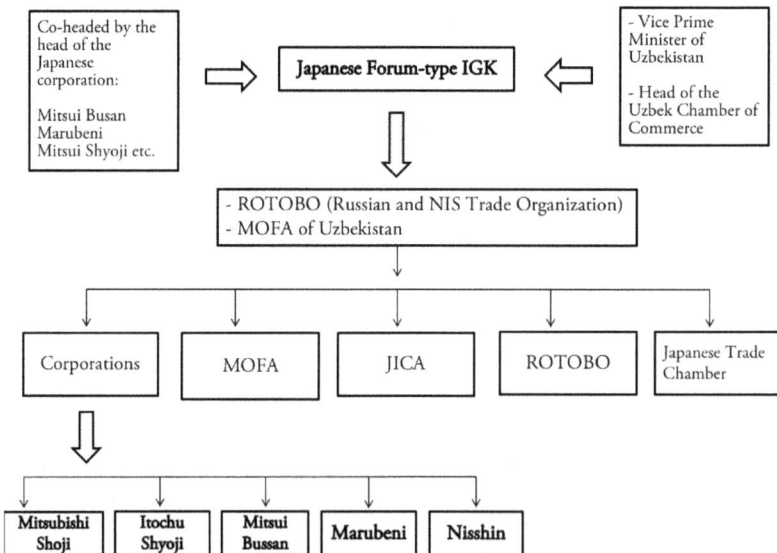

Although the logic of this structure is that the committee becomes a meeting place between Japanese businesses and Uzbek bureaucracy, in practice, these meetings do not result in expected outcomes because these actors operate with different objectives. While the Uzbek bureaucracy operates on behalf of the government, the Japanese side aims at airing corporate voices, which are not connected to policy. In many cases, these committees turn into forum-type meetings that articulate many desirable objectives but produce very few tangible outcomes.

As is often the case, entrepreneurs frequently express desires to enter certain markets and areas, including in Uzbekistan, but unless the conditions are prepared in terms of the legal and financial infrastructure, the Japanese corporate community displays a significant degree of hesitance in entering such markets, despite strong governmental support in facilitating such entry. This is perhaps the greatest difference in Japanese and Chinese corporate behaviors because Chinese corporations seek to compensate for the absence of legal and financial infrastructures through agreements between the governments that provide additional guarantees to the corporations entering Uzbekistan.

With regard to Japanese and Korean corporate behavior, certain similarities exist between the two. However, Korean entrepreneurs seek to utilize the opportunities received in the negotiations during governments' official visits, and if those agreements do not materialize well many Korean companies immediately withdraw without hesitation. Therefore, the Chinese approach represents "high risk compensated by governmental guarantees," while Korean corporate behavior can be summarized as "high risk, high return versus low return, fast retreat" and the Japanese behavior is closer to the model of "no risk, low/no return."

The composition of these countries' interstate economic cooperation committees with Uzbekistan significantly influences the outcomes of deliberations. In line with the above explanations, intergovernmental economic cooperation plans between China and Uzbekistan are heavily dominated by the projects implemented by private enterprises in the fields that remain of high interest to both the Chinese and Uzbek governments. Therefore, one can observe the invisible hand of both governments in guiding their enterprises into the fields they consider important for state development. In the case of the Japan-Uzbek commission, one can observe the dominance of intergovernmental agreements and commitments, mainly because the Japanese enterprises have not yet expressed an overwhelming commitment to involvement in projects in Uzbekistan. Thus, the majority of roadmaps consist of framework agreements between the two governments and mutual understanding memorandums and agreements regarding Official Development Assistance projects.

In the Korean case, as explained above, the agenda for cooperation is defined by only a few documents, such as the Strategic Partnership Agreement between Uzbekistan and Korea (2018–20) and the Uzbek Development Strategy (2017–21).

Figure 8. Korea-Uzbek Interstate Economic Cooperation Committee Composition

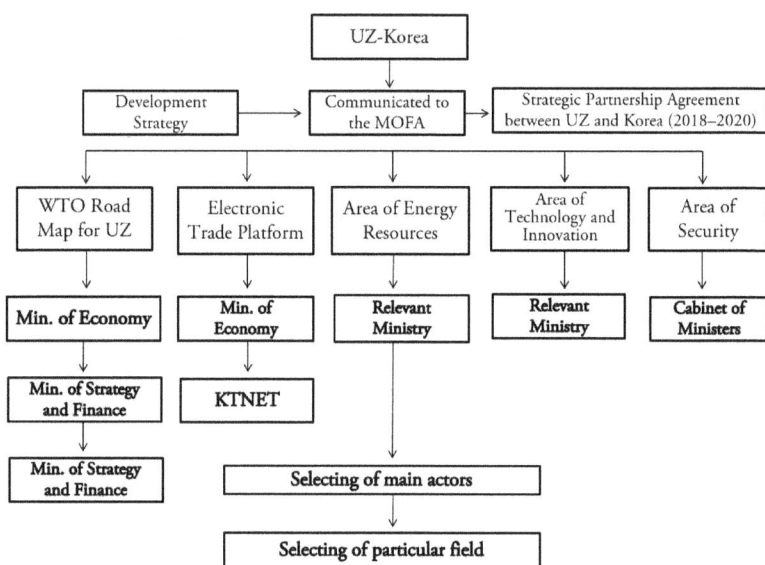

Few areas aside from active Korean entrepreneurial activities are the focus of cooperation between the two countries. One is the road-map for assisting Uzbekistan to join the World Trade Organization (WTO), with Korea's invaluable assistance in setting up electronic trade and e-governance platforms in Uzbekistan as well as areas of human resource development. Cooperation in these areas was so successful that a number of Korean nationals were appointed to the Uzbek Cabinet of Ministers at the rank of deputy minister to supervise and implement reforms in these areas. This is a significant development for the CA region because few cases exist in which regional countries, and especially Uzbekistan, open their governmental structures to recruit foreign nationals for ministerial positions. Korea in this sense is considered somewhat of a "safe bet" because it possesses the required expertise yet displays understanding toward authoritarian governance, as Korea itself has experienced the transition from a dictatorship to a democracy.

Figure 9. Korea-Uzbek Roadmap Agreements and Composition (USD billion)

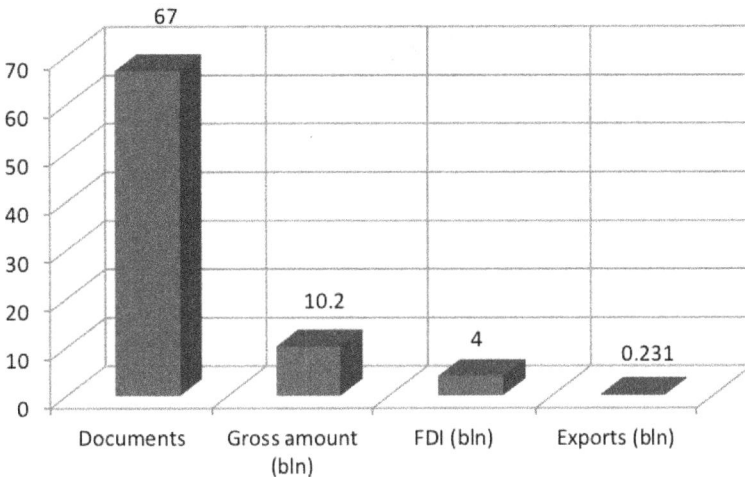

Note: The figures are for a total of 67 documents.

The areas covered in the agreements that became the roadmap of economic cooperation are dispersed across very wide areas of coverage. Each area outlined in Figure 10 is composed of a number of agreements, each of which aims at smaller objectives and is often implemented by a different actor. Therefore, the roadmap of cooperation with Korea in its essence is more dense and complicated when compared with the Japanese roadmap. It might not be as significant in terms of the overall amount covered by its projects when compared to the one with China, but in terms of project diversity and actor multiplicity, it supersedes the latter.

Figure 10. The Areas and Projects of Cooperation Included in the Korea-Uzbek Roadmap of Cooperation

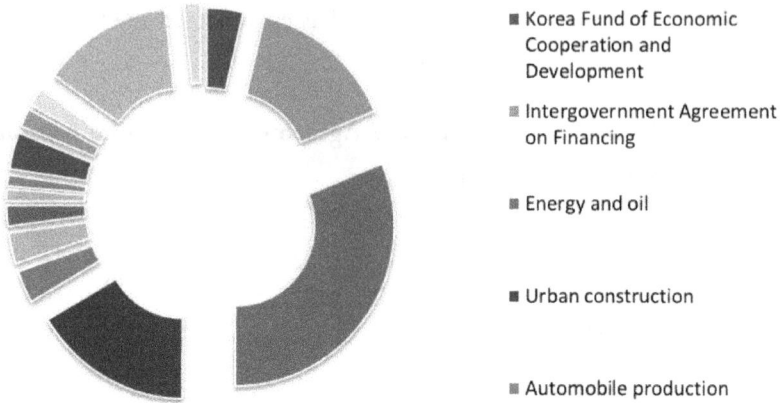

- Korea Fund of Economic Cooperation and Development
- Intergovernment Agreement on Financing
- Energy and oil
- Urban construction
- Automobile production

China's Inroads into the Infrastructure, Resource, and Manufacturing Sectors

Two main areas are covered in the China-Uzbek economic cooperation roadmaps. These are infrastructure and resources, and manufacturing/export-oriented industries. The largest economic infrastructure-related agreements concluded between China and Uzbekistan as a part of the economic cooperation roadmap are those focusing on the joint production of synthetic fuel, investment in Uzbekistan's oil industry, prospective new projects, cooperation in the construction of energy generation plants, railroad infrastructure development, and Tashkent to Osh (Kyrgyzstan) road construction.

Figure 11. China-Uzbek Roadmap-Related Project Areas (USD billion)

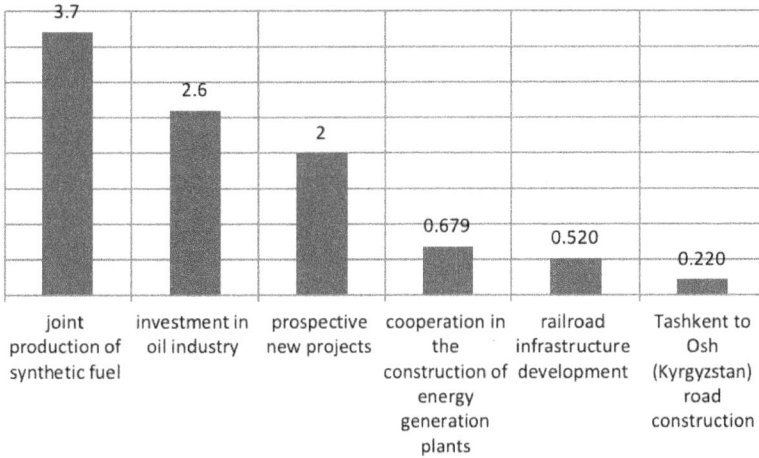

In terms of establishing manufacturing lines in Uzbekistan, agreements were reached on establishing production facilities for cement, textiles, electric appliances, metals, and glass.

Figure 12. China-Uzbek Roadmap-Related Production Facilities (USD million)

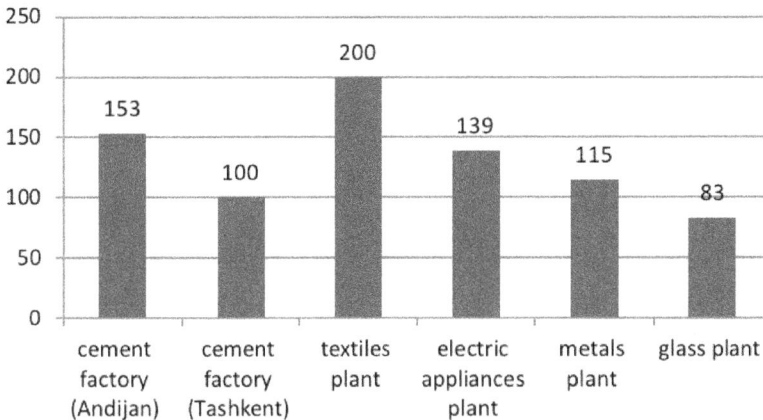

One of the most significant infrastructure agreements, signed in May 2017, was between Uzbekistan and the PRC on facilitating smooth international road transportation between the two countries, which involves the simplification of procedures and the creation of an environment to increase the transportation of goods using land roads. This agreement followed all the internal procedures in Uzbekistan and has been confirmed by decree of the president ("Decree of the President of Uzbekistan" 2017).[31]

The project, which aims to connect China with Uzbekistan through the territory of the Kyrgyz Republic, has also been addressed in relevant signed agreements. It would connect the Uzbek city of Andijan and the Chinese city of Kashgar, via Osh and Irkeshtam in Kyrgyzstan, by both rail and motor road. This is the shortest route, and both countries are interested in its construction. [32] While China has for years been interested in a number of transport corridors to European markets through CA's transport networks, these particular rail and motor roads are of particular interest and importance to Uzbekistan. They would allow Uzbekistan to shorten the distance to transport its goods into China by avoiding Kazakh railroads, which take longer and cost more. The new rail and motor roads would allow Uzbekistan to ship its goods directly, using the shortest route to China through Kyrgyzstan.

In 2012, Kyrgyzstan drafted its own railroad project. It would cover more areas of Kyrgyzstan and be 380 km longer than the current rail system. For Kyrgyzstan, it would be a chance to develop its own railroad system and connect remote areas that the rail system currently bypasses. However, for both Uzbekistan and China this project would entail a longer transportation time for their cargo and much higher costs for the project in general. The plans suggested by Kyrgyzstan appear to be difficult for China and Uzbekistan to accept.[33]

Both Chinese and Uzbek officials realize that a certain degree of caution is required with respect to Chinese infrastructure projects, so they need public engagement and awareness. To facilitate public acceptance of this project, the Chinese and Uzbek governments agreed to organize an auto rally along the route of the future railroad, which serves several important goals. First, it aims to promote to the public the transportation infrastructure development projects between Chinese and Central Asian counterparts. Second, it is a practical test of the preparedness of areas where railroad construction is planned to determine any issues in the terrain and detail the infrastructure-related facilities that must be constructed in this area. In addition to the railroad, the Chinese Railway Tunnel Group, which built the 19-kilometer Kamchik Tunnel in Uzbekistan, has committed to the construction of a vehicle motorway under the tunnel, naming the project Kamchik 2 ("China to Help Build" 2017).[34]

Uzbekistan's exports of mineral and natural resources to China constitute a considerable share of the trade between the countries. According to other agreements concluded in May 2017 during Mirziyoyev's visit to China, contracts were signed for natural gas (6 billion m3), uranium, textiles, leather, and agricultural products to be exported to China by the end of 2017. Plans have also been articulated for exports of natural gas to reach USD 2.4 billion for the years 2018 to 2020 ("Uzbekistan planiruet k 2021" 2017).[35]

Figure 13. China-Uzbek Roadmap-Related Plans for Resource Exports (USD million)

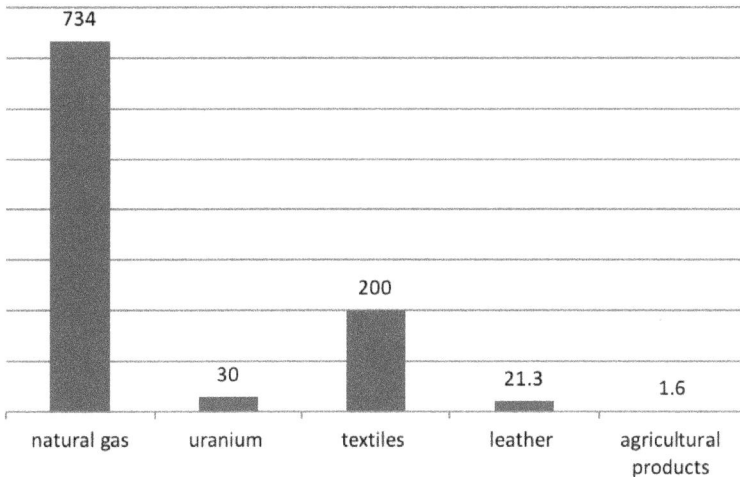

Discussions were also held regarding new pipelines that would connect natural gas endowed Turkmenistan, Uzbekistan, and Kazakhstan to Chinese consumers to ensure a stable supply. However, no construction plans or financial commitments have yet been achieved due to uncertainties regarding the economic sustainability of the pipelines' operations.

Chinese companies, such as Shengli Oil and Freet Petroleum, represent strategic partners for the government and related corporations in the provision of pipes and other extraction equipment. According to sources aware of the negotiations between the government and Chinese corporations, at least three contracts for the supply of such equipment were signed during Mirziyoyev's visit to Beijing in 2017.

China National Petroleum Corporation secured a co-financing contract from the Bank of China for a project for drilling at the gas condensate field in Bukhara, Uzbekistan, by establishing JV New Silk Road Oil and Gas, which was set up by Uzbekneftegaz and China National Oil and Gas Exploration and Development Corporation (a subsidiary of China National Petroleum Corporation) ("Uzbekistan-China JV" 2017).[36] According to the license granted to the joint venture, it plans to develop the existing wells and drill another 16, with annual production to reach 1 billion m3 of natural gas and 6,500 tons of condensate (ibid.).[37]

In terms of the generation of new industries, Uzbekistan concluded an agreement between Uzbekneftegaz and the Chinese Development Bank (worth USD 3.7 billion, of which USD 1.2 billion is to be financed by China) to finance the establishment of a plant to produce synthetic fuel at Uzbekistan's largest gas refinery complex, Shurtan.[38] The plant would process 3.6 billion m3 of natural gas into 743,000 tons of synthetic fuel; 311,000 tons of aviation fuel; 431,000 tons of naphtha fuel; and 20,900 tons of liquefied gas ("Uzbekistan i Kitai podpisali" 2017).[39] Technological support for the plant is to be provided by South Korea's Hyundai Engineering and Construction under a license provided by South African Sasol. The technology for turning natural gas into liquefied gas would come from Dutch Haldor Topsoe.

A USD 3 billion agreement between the Chinese Ministry of Commerce and Uzbekgidro stipulates the modernization of approximately 300 water pump stations to improve the efficiency of Uzbekistan's hydroelectricity sector.[40] Uzbekistan developed and approved the strategy for hydro energy development in November 2015 and aims to invest USD 889.4 million in the sector between 2016 and 2020. The modernization of 15 hydroelectric stations is planned, to allow the generation of 5.25 billion kilowatts of energy.

This governmental program was essential in defining this area as a high priority in relations with China.

Modernization of energy generation in Uzbekistan has also been prioritized in negotiations. In particular, the China Railway Tunnel Group and the China Coal Technology and Engineering Group began modernizing a plant to extract 900,000 tons of coal per year, with the investment of USD 94.5 million ("Startovala modernizatsiya predpriyatiya" 2017).[41] Nontraditional sustainable sources such as biomass generation have also been the subject of agreements. Uzbekneftegaz, AKB Agrobank, and China's Poly International Holdings signed a memorandum of cooperation to set up the production of a modern biogas plants worth USD 10 million and to assist in the modernization of eight domestic enterprises, including the Plant Oil and Gas and Chemical Engineering, JSC, in line with the governmental Program of Measures to Increase Biogas Plants in Uzbekistan for 2017–19 (Tashkent Times 2017).[42] Last but not least, solid waste processing infrastructure is being constructed to improve livelihoods and facilitate better waste utilization in both old and newly constructed quarters in Uzbekistan (Beston Machinery Company).[43]

The second area targeted by the China-Uzbek economic cooperation roadmaps is the area of manufacturing and export-oriented industry development. As described above, the new administration in Uzbekistan has defined certain areas in which China's economic presence and technology are desirable and advantageous. In line with the goals of the development strategy, the first such area is the establishment of small- and medium-sized manufacturing plants to not only supplement imported products but also, importantly, produce goods that can compete in Central Asian markets.

Uzbekistan intends to establish long-term cooperation with the Chinese Aerospace Science and Industry Corporation (CASIC) for the supply of scanning equipment

In particular, Uzbekistan intends to establish long-term cooperation with the Chinese Aerospace Science and Industry Corporation (CASIC) for the supply of scanning equipment for border control services, customs, airports, and rail infrastructure, the introduction of urban security systems ("smart city"), the protection of large facilities and the border, the development and introduction of an industrial Internet, joint production of a wide range of pharmaceuticals in Uzbekistan, and CASIC's participation in the development of infrastructure for the Central Military Clinical Hospital of the Ministry of Defense. This latter project includes creating a turnkey multidisciplinary medical and diagnostic building and equipping it with modern medical equipment, as well as producing oil and gas equipment.[44]

To respond to the increasing demand for construction materials, the Uzbek government intends to facilitate the development of a cement plant (with Zhejiang Shangfeng Building Materials, at a cost of USD 203.9 million) ("New Cement Plant" 2017)[45] and glass production (with MingYuan Silu, at a cost of USD 110 million) ("Glass Production Plant" 2017).[46] Another joint venture has been established in the city of Gulistan, focusing on the production of elevators. In the Soviet era, Uzbekistan relied heavily on elevators produced in other republics, namely, Azerbaijan and Russia. With the collapse of the Soviet Union, the replacement of installed elevators required importing them in great numbers. To fill this gap and respond to the increasing need for elevators in the booming construction business in Uzbekistan, the government sought China's assistance in facilitating the production of elevators in Uzbekistan. As a result, a joint venture for the production of elevators (Modern Lift Systems) has been established in the Syrdarya Region of Uzbekistan, funded by Chinese investors and using Chinese technology. It produces 300 elevators per year, plus 200 escalators and travelators (moving walkways). Although the joint venture produces elevators for internal consumption, approximately 30 percent of its products are exported to other regional states ("Proizvodtsvo liftov zapuscheno" 2017).[47]

In terms of memoranda and protocols, some of these have already materialized in production facilities, such as the one for the production of soft and hard toys in Tashkent, based on the Soviet-era toy factory Tashkentigrushka ("O merakh po organizatsii" 2017).[48] As mentioned, Uzbekistan is the most populous country in CA, and 60 percent of its 32 million people are under 25 years old (2017 data). The population has the highest growth rate in CA, which creates a large market for toys and child-related products. In the Soviet era,

Uzbekistan hosted one of the region's largest toy factories. However, with the collapse of the Soviet Union and aging technology, the plant was unable to meet the needs of the market. The quality of toys imported from other countries, including China, was at the level expected by consumers, motivating the government to seek a solution. Toy imports reached USD 2.1 million in 2016 but fell 29 percent in 2017 due to increasing local production. As mentioned, 94 percent (USD 2 million) of the toys imported into Uzbekistan are from China; Russia's share is only 2.1 percent (USD 43,000), with the remaining 0.8 percent (USD 16,000) coming from Lithuania ("Uzbekistan and China Will Create" 2017).[49] The new factory (jointly established with Shandong Sanhe Toy) cost an estimated USD 23 million; makes 700 kinds of plastic, soft, electronic, and mechanical toys and provides 950 jobs in Tashkent.[50]

The majority of these projects attempt to establish production and infrastructure-related facilities to enable Uzbekistan to produce goods not only for its large (but still limited) internal consumption but also, importantly, for export. The toy factory aims to produce seven million individual toys annually, of which 80 percent are meant for export to other countries of CA, Russia, Afghanistan, and beyond. Similar plants are also planned in conjunction with other Chinese producers (such as Zhejiang Jiyou) in the Jizzakh free economic area ("Zhejiang Jiyou Industrial" 2017).[51]

Similar protocols for intentions to establish production plants for ceramics with Peng Yu Special Ceramics and Zhongguo Jingdezhen Porcelain and a porcelain production plant with Ru Hong have been signed ("FEZ 'Angren'" 2017).[52] Although the documents signed with representatives of these companies were protocols of intention without firm commitments, in June and July 2017 the representatives visited possible sites for plant construction and discussed conditions with various ministries, such as the Ministry of Foreign Trade, the Foreign Investment Agency, and the State Committee for Competition Controls.

Among the agreements signed between the two countries, Sun Paper Industry and China National Complete Plant Import and Export signed a protocol of intentions with the government to create a cluster for the production of high-quality paper in the Angren free economic zone ("COMPLANT planiruet organizovat'" 2017).[53]

Uzbekistan currently does not have such facilities and needs to import much of the high-quality paper used in office paperwork and for wrapping and shipping the goods produced in various plants ("V Uzbekistane budet sozdano" 2017).[54] Delegations from these companies visited Uzbekistan in September 2017 to evaluate the needs and to coordinate equipment supplies with local counterparts.

In terms of the export of Uzbek-made products, the agreements signed during President Mirziyoyev's May 2017 visit included textile exports (USD 300 million) and leather (USD 60 million) and agricultural products (USD 1.6 million) in 2017–18. These contracts are in active implementation, and the majority are being implemented. Additionally, cotton-processing and textile mills have been planned, with Chinese participation, in the Qashqadaryo Region for 2017–19. Seven textile mills are under construction in Qashqadaryo, and their overall cotton-processing capacity will account for 10 percent of the annual cotton output of the Qashqadaryo Region ("Uzbekistan President Visits Litai" 2017).[55] The Litai project aims to create 500 jobs using textile machinery from the Saurer Group and to produce 22,000 tons of high-level cotton yarn annually, 80 percent for export (ibid.).[56] Wenzhou Jinsheng Trading announced that it will initiate seven investment projects in the Jizzakh economic zone, investing USD 40 million in reprocessing local resources and producing leather goods and metal products, one-third of which are to be exported out of Uzbekistan ("Kitaj pomozhet realizovat" 2017).[57]

> *Wenzhou Jinsheng Trading announced that it will invest USD 40 million in the Jizzakh economic zone*

Korea's Inroads into Uzbekistan

As mentioned in the previous section, to better understand its essence, the Uzbek-Korean cooperation roadmap can be conceptually divided into several consistent parts. First, the roadmap includes several framework agreements between governments and plans for the co-financing of projects. In particular, the Korean government extended the grant (USD 500 million through the Export-Import Bank of Korea (Korea Eximbank) to finance the projects that are agreed upon in consultations between the two governments. Similarly, both governments agreed to provide financing to the projects, which are to be jointly selected with the participation of experts from both governments (with a budget of USD 2 billion for 2018–20).

Figure 14. Agreements Included in Korea-Uzbek Roadmaps on Finance-Related Plans

Financing	
Eksimbank of Korea (USD 150 million).	Loan for financing of financing of various projects
«GST Korea» (USD 20 million).	Loan for leasing of specialized machinery of «Hyundai Heavy Industries»
«Road International Co. Ltd» (USD 10 million).	
«KCP» (USD 10 million).	Loan for leasing of cement-making machinery
«KwangShin» (USD 10 million).	Loan for leasing of gas fueling station
Eksimbank of Korea (USD 65 million).	Credit line for financing of projects
Eksimbank of Korea (USD 30 million).	Additional loan agreement

Second, the roadmap aims to provide nonfinancial assistance and support to Uzbekistan. In particular, both governments developed a coordinated set of actions and roadmaps for assisting Uzbekistan in joining the World Trade Organization. These measures include provisions of consultation and Korean expertise in preparing for Uzbekistan's entry into the WTO. Such entry benefits not only Uzbekistan but, importantly, also assists Korean entry into the Uzbek market, making such assistance to Uzbekistan an important objective for Korean expansion into Uzbekistan. In addition to such intergovernmental framework agreements, a few agreements on expertise exchange were signed by various ministries and state agencies. In particular, Uzbekistan's Ministry of Economy and Korea's Ministry of Strategy and Finance signed a memorandum on the exchange of know-how regarding the evaluation and selection of goals for development ("Korea and Uzbekistan Agree" 2018).[58]

Figure 15. Nontrade Support and Assistance Agreements between Korea and Uzbekistan

	Visits
	Visits
1	Organization of the visit by the President of Korea Moon in 2018
2	Preparing a visit of PM in 2018
3	Preparing a visit by FM in early 2018 and holding round of negotiations between MOFAs
4	Participation in 11th Forum of Republic of Korea-Central Asia in 2018
	Inter-parliament exchange
5	Preparing a visit of the Speaker of the Legislative Chamber of Parliament of Uzbekistan to Korea
6	Intensification of activities of parliamentarian "groups of friendship" and ties
7	Setting up the meeting of Vice PM in Uzbekistan
	Business forums
8	Uzbek Korean Intergovernmental committee for economic (trade-economic) cooperation in Uzb.
9	Holding regular business forums under the auspices of PMs
10	Creation of working group on the Most preferable trade partner status in Uzb-Korean trade
11	Creation of chapter to support Korean businesses under the auspices of Uzb. Chamber of Commerce
12	Increase of annual trade volume to 3 billion USD in the nearest years (uranium, metals, agricultural products, construction materials, chemical and oil products
13	Implementation of 24 export contracts for USD 231 million
14	Improvements in the functioning of Navoi logistics center
15	Setting up a long-term cooperation between quarantine services
16	Establishing representative office of Agency on foreign labor migration of Uzbekistan in Kwanju
	In cultural fields
17	Opening a Korean culture house in Tashkent
18	Creating a Museum of Korean Diaspora in Uzbekistan
19	Renaming one of the central streets in Tashkent after city of Seoul
20	Establishing a recreational park named after city of Seoul
21	Hiring a specialist from the city mayor's office of Seoul as a consultant for mayor of Tashkent

In educational fields	
22	Organization of long-term cooperation with «Myongji Hospital».
23	Creating of clinics of Chong in Tashkent.
24	Setting up cooperation between Min. of Healthcare and Gachon University Gil Medical Center
25	Organization of visits of medical doctors from Chonnam University and holding master classes
26	Appointing the general director of Chonnam University into honorary Executive Adviser of Ministry of Healthcare of Uzbekistan
27	Training of healthcare specialists in the clinics of Korea
28	Visits by members of Association of Prominent Medical Specialists of Korea with master classes
29	Organization of charity medical events for children with born defects and disabilities
30	Discussions opening up a Korean University branch on urbanization, architecture and city design
31	Organization of joint experimental smart kindergartens with the fund «AI COREA»
32	Seminars on pre-school education with faculty of Sangmyong, Chonnam, Chung and Korea Univ.
33	Implementation of agreement on transfer of from «Booyoung» company of 2000 electrical pianos for educational institutions of Uzbekistan (Korean side delivers the pianos to the nearest sea port from where the Uzbek side provides transportation costs to Uzbekistan).

A similar memorandum was signed by both countries' ministries of justice. In terms of some tangible knowledge transfer for use by entrepreneurs, Uzbekistan's government reached an agreement with relevant actors, such as the Korea Trade Network (KTNET), on assistance in the development and introduction of a national electronic trade platform using the Korean experience. In line with this agreement, experts from KTNET will assist the Uzbek government in preparing the platform for internet-based trade, and, once the proposal is agreed upon by the Uzbek government, the request for funding will be submitted to one of the Korean financial institutions.[59]

Third, such a trade platform for Uzbekistan needs to be prepared because Uzbek agricultural and industrial producers are often cut off from domestic and international consumers due to logistical problems related to connecting demand and supply. In many instances, producers have to rely on personal connections and "word of a mouth" in finding their trading partners. Cooperation with Korea aims to alleviate this problem by connecting Uzbek and Korean producers and consumers in direct contractual relations across various areas such as energy, agriculture, and urban construction, as indicated in the tables below.

Figure 16. Number of Cooperation Documents in Various Areas between Uzbekistan and Korea

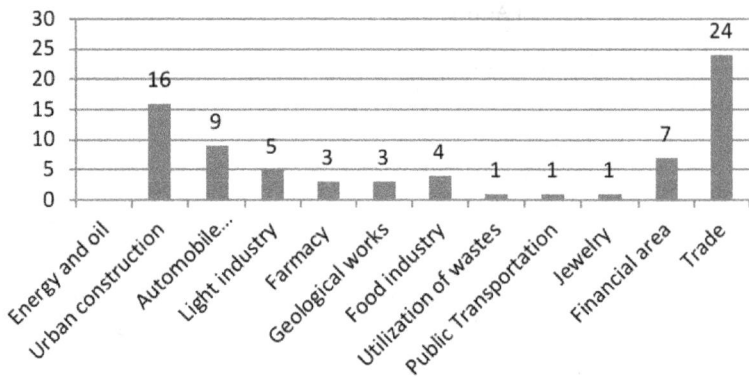

Figure 17. Uzbek-Korean Trade and Investment Related Agreements (USD billion)

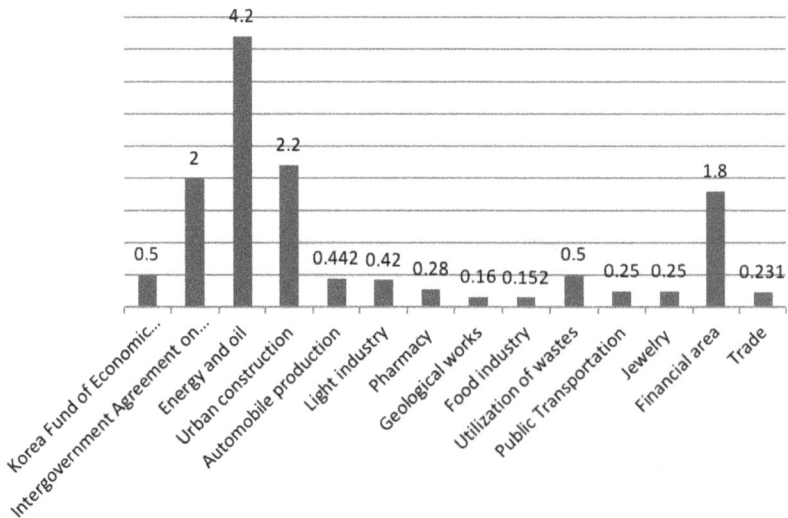

As can also be seen in the figures below, the contracts include clearly defined products and amounts to be invested in these areas by Korean and Uzbek counterparts. The roadmap also details the companies' names, their expected investment amounts, and the expected outcome of such cooperation. While not all of these materialize, they represent a very concrete and focused approach to the facilitation of interaction between the private enterprises.

Figure 18. Uzbek-Korean Agreements in Energy, Oil, and Chemistry

Energy, Oil and Chemistry field – 15 documents (USD 4.2 billion)		
1	Consortium of «POSCO Daewoo» and «Hyundai Engineering and Construction» – (USD 1.8 billion)	3 projects: Construction of Heat Electric Stations (Navoi, Tahiatash and modernization of Bukhara, Samarkand and Jizzakh HES
2	Sprott Korea Corp. (USD 1 billion).	Construction of Solar Energy Stations (1000 Mvt) (2018–2019)
3	«Samsung Engineering» (USD 106 million)	Modernization of Fergana Azot factory
4	«SK Engineering and Construction» (USD 250 million).	Processing of garbage
5	«GS Engineering & Construction» (USD 200 million).	Processing of 250 thousand tons of methanol into gasoline using MTG
6	«POSCO Daewoo» (USD 127,5 million).	Production of solar panel modules
7	«Seoul Electronics & Telecom Co.ltd» (USD 50 million).	Production of energy efficient lamps
8	«Kiturami» (USD 50 million)	Production of heating grids
9	«KNOC» (USD 24.5 million).	Search drilling on Dekhkanabad and Tashkurgan sites
10	«Winhousing» (USD 4.2 million).	Production of wall paper on Ferghana Azot plant
11	«Jeil Architecture» (USD 1 million).	Production of floor heating equipment
12	«Daesung Celyic Enersys» (USD 1 million).	Production of heating grids
13	«Capital Industrial Development Co. Ltd.» (USD 10 million).	Production of motor oil

Energy, Oil and Chemistry field – 15 documents (USD 4.2 billion)	
14	«NK Group» (USD 2 million).	JV for maintenance of stationary and mobile Natural Gas Compressor Stations.

Figure 19. Uzbek-Korean Agreements and Contracts in the Fields of Building and Construction, Machinery Production, Chemistry, and Agriculture

Building and construction		
15	«Hyundai Engineering» (USD 1 million).	Processing of natural gas, value-added production
16	«POSCO Daewoo» (USD 1.4 billion).	«High Tech City» construction in Tashkent
17	«G&W Co Ltd.» (USD 280 million).	«Tashkent city» business center construction
18	«Leaders Country Club Co., Ltd.» (USD 70 million).	Golf field and housing construction in Tashkent
19	«Keumdo Group Co. Ltd» (USD 8 million).	Housing construction
20	«Jeil Construction» (USD 6 million).	Construction of eco-village in the Tashkent region
21	«GEO 2 Co., Ltd.» (USD 3 million).	Creation of digital city inventory of buildings in Tashkent
22	«Triniti International Inc.» (USD 2.7 million).	«Tashkent Lakeside Golf Club» construction
23	«Khil Pyung Co. Ltd» (USD 7 million).	Housing construction in Sergeli district of Tashkent
24	Evergreen Holdings» (USD 300 million).	Cement production plant
25	«SY Panel Co. Ltd.» (USD 50 million).	Production of construction panels
26	«IL KWANG E&C», «HCND» (USD 50 million).	Housing construction
27	«Hyundai Department Store Group» (USD 20 million).	Construction of logistics center for construction machinery

28	«erae cs limited» (USD 20 million).	Production of painting materials
29	«Evergreen Holdings» (USD 10 million).	Processing of mineral stones
30	«OJOO Tech» (USD 4 million).	Production of Medium-density fibreboard
31	«Nurichem Co. Ltd.» (USD 2 million).	Production of construction hermetic materials
Machinery production		
32	«Evergreen Motors» (USD 200 million).	Production of «Hyundai» machinery
33	JV with «Everdigm» (USD 3 million).	Production of specialized machinery «Everdigm»
34	«GM Korea» (USD 143.8 million).	Production of new line of the car (Tracker)
35	«GM Korea» (USD 25 million).	Production of new type of engine (1.8 l.c)
36	«GM Korea» (USD 15 million).	Production of modernized version of Cobalt
37	«Dong Kwang Group» (USD 3 million).	Production of motorcycles and tricycles
38	«Erae» (USD 1.7 million).	Production of ventilation and heating systems for automobiles
39	«GW International» (USD 1.1 million).	Production of plasmatic parts of automobiles
40	«Youngone Corp» (USD 25 million).	Production of sewing machines in Tashkent and Samarkand
41	«DAEWON CO.» (USD 10 million).	Production of textiles for school uniforms
42	«Samwon Ind. Co., Ltd.» (USD 2.5 million).	Production of textile paints
43	«Textile Technologies Group» (2 stage) (USD 1.8 million).	Production of textile paints
Chemistry		
44	«Erae» (USD 20 million).	Production of medical components
45	«Dalim Biotech» (USD 5 million).	Production of antidiabetic medicines

46	«Yuhan» (USD 3 million).	Production of medical components
47	«Shindong Resources» (USD 10 million).	Industrial gold production
48	«Shindong Resources» (USD 3 million).	Industrial wolfram production
49	«Hanjin D&B Equipment» (USD 3 million).	Production of drilling equipment
Agriculture		
50	«Erae» (USD 60 million).	Construction of logistics center for agricultural products
51	«Erae» (USD 60 million).	Production of indoor agricultural production
52	«Human & Idea Co. Ltd.» (USD 20 million).	Poultry facilities construction
53	«CIELIE Co.» (USD 12 million).	Processing of agricultural products
54	«SEJIN G&E» (USD 50 million).	Waste utilization and management
55	«LG CNS» (USD 25 million).	Public Transportation Management (TOPIS)
56	«Hwachon Plant—Gemco» (USD 30 million).	Production of jewelry
57	«AVID» (USD 5 million).	Production of jewelry

Figure 20. Uzbek-Korean Export Contracts on Particular Products

Contract for delivery of uranium for USD **72 million**
Contract for delivery of cotton textile for USD **12 million**
Contract for delivery of beans for USD **1 million**
Contract for delivery of 2000 ton of medium for USD **13 million**
Contract for delivery of 1000 ton of agricultural products for USD **3 million**
Framework agreement for delivery for 3000 ton of medium for USD **19.5 million**
Contract for delivery of cherry for USD **2 million**
Contract for delivery of 2000 ton of beans for USD **1.6 million**
Contract for delivery of 600 ton of pomegranate for USD **600,000**
Contract for delivery of beans and cherry for USD **10 million**
Uzbekengilsanoat - 12 contracts for USD 94.3 million
Contracts (5) for delivery of cherry for and textile for USD **2.45 million**

Contracts (3) for delivery of cotton textile for USD **61.4 million**
Contracts for delivery of textile products for USD **15.4 million**
Contract for textile products for USD **14.8 thousand**
Contract for delivery of silk нитей for the USD **400,000**
Agreement for joint sells of textile products for USD **30 million**
Contract for delivery of leather for USD **2 million**

Uzbekistan's Ministry of Employment and Labor Resources of Uzbekistan and Ministry of Personnel Management have concluded a memorandum on cooperation in labor resource management addressing the matter of abundant labor resources (the number of unemployed people seeking employment in Korea or elsewhere that exceeds needs domestically) in Uzbekistan. In particular, this memorandum is expected to provide some management of the uncontrolled labor migration from Uzbekistan to Korea. While Korea displays openness in accepting such laborers, the Korean side is concerned about illegally employed laborers frequently overstaying their legal permits. Connected to such memorandums is the range of agreements within the cooperation roadmap that aim for the opening of educational and vocational training institutions in Uzbekistan by Korean universities and institutions. These are agreements on opening a branch of Pohan Polytechnic University (agreement with POSCO Daewoo) and a branch of Ajou University with a medical clinic; an agreement between the Ministry of Healthcare of Uzbekistan and the Medical Leaders Corporation of Korea; a "roadmap" signed by the Korean Institute of Rare Metals (KIRAM) on cooperation in scientific, technical, and innovation activities with the Ministry of Foreign Trade of Uzbekistan and on training and exchange of expertise with the Almalyk Mountain Metallurgical Plant ("Uzbekistan and South Korea Sign Documents" 2017);[60] and agreements on cooperation in training personnel for geological works with Chonnam National University and on the creation of a joint institute with the Korean Research Institute of Chemical Technology (KRICT) ("Uzbekistan and KRICT" 2017).[61]

Japanese Roadmaps into Uzbekistan

Certain features stand out in reading through the roadmap of economic cooperation between Japan and Uzbekistan. The first feature is the importance of government-to-government cooperation in relations between the two countries. To some extent, this feature again confirms the importance of the style of governance and international cooperation in the CA region, especially in Uzbekistan. Although styles of governance differ between Japan and Uzbekistan, governments remain important in paving the way for international cooperation and defining the degree of success of international engagement for Uzbekistan. With regard to the hesitance displayed by the Japanese corporate community, the Japanese government and its assistance schemes stand out as the most important factor of the Japanese foreign policy engagement in CA and Uzbekistan. In this sense, Japan has historically been active and has provided significant amounts of ODA assistance, which was crucial for Uzbekistan's economic survival, especially in the early years of its independence (the early 1990s). This pattern of Japanese engagement, using ODA as the main tool for its influence in this region, is also reflected in the latest roadmaps between Japan and Uzbekistan. In contrast to the Chinese and Korean roadmaps, which include a significant number of projects featuring private companies and enterprises, the Japanese roadmap of cooperation with Uzbekistan contains mostly projects and initiatives in which the Japanese government plays the most important role. Structurally, these roadmaps can be divided into two main parts. The first part consists of the roadmaps of cooperation aiming to facilitate smooth interaction between both countries' governments and governmental agencies, as is demonstrated in Figure 21.

Figure 21. Uzbek-Japanese Roadmaps of Intergovernmental Interaction

No.	Planned Interaction	Main actors	Essence
Political Field			
1	Facilitation of the first visit of President Mirziyoyev to Japan.	MOFA, MEECAT	Invitation received from FM Kishida during 6th Central Asia Plus Japan Dialogue forum in Turkmenistan
2	Implementation of the strategic partnership between Uzbekistan and Japan concluded during the visit of PM Abe to Uzbekistan, October 24–26, 2015.	MOFA, MEECAT	Bilateral negotiations at the level of embassies, MOFA, etc. Few tangible outcomes though.
3	Facilitation of cooperation between MOFA of Uzbekistan and Japan 2015–2017.	MOFA, MEECAT	16th and 17th round of political consultations in Tokyo and Tashkent.
4	Inter-parliamentary interactions and facilitation of the 2nd inter-parliamentary cooperation meeting.	MOFA, Oliy Majlis, Diet	Deliberations with Japanese Parliamentary League of Friendship with Uzbekistan about holding the forum in Tashkent
5	Facilitation of inter-MOFA political consultations.	MOFA	November 2017, Tashkent (planned)
6	Participation of delegation of Uzbekistan in the 6th Central Asia Plus Japan Dialogue forum in Turkmenistan.	MOFA, MEECAT, Ministry of Water Management	May 1, 2017
7	Review of legal documents related to the cooperation between Uzbekistan and Japan.	MOFA, related agencies	Review is planned for the second half of 2017

Intergovernmental cooperation has historically been the strong area in relations between the two countries. Japan is a country that has historically been welcomed to the CA region. Its colonial and imperial history in the East Asian context is not well known or relevant to the CA context. Thus, CA, and Uzbekistan, in particular, remains one of the most Japan-friendly regions and countries in the world judging from a number of public polls conducted from the mid-2000s to 2015. The relative distance of Japan from the CA region, its ODA assistance, and the egalitarian way its companies treat the local workforce (especially when compared to the Chinese corporations, which tend to bring a Chinese labor force and discriminate against local workers) create a significant expectation from the local business community and population for Japan's wider involvement in this region. However, as featured in the first part of the roadmaps and displayed in the activities envisaged in Figure 21, intergovernmental contacts (as opposed to private enterprises) remain the largest driver of cooperation between the two countries. Accordingly, these activities focus on facilitating the visit to Tokyo of Mirziyoyev, the newly elected president of Uzbekistan, meetings of foreign ministers, participation within multilateral forums such as Central Asia plus Japan and reconfirming the framework agreements and other legal documents stipulating relations between the two countries. These types of activities are conducted between Uzbekistan and most of its foreign partners. However, they also demonstrate that, although Japan has been very active in the field of Official Development Assistance and has provided much-needed and appreciated educational grants, much room remains for the expansion of political activities into the field of economic interactions.

As seen in Figure 22, many attempts have been made to revitalize economic cooperation between the two countries, which currently lags far behind the Japanese advances in the fields of political dialogue and humanitarian assistance. Regular meetings within the joint economic cooperation committee and attempts to initiate various business forums (cotton, textile, and agricultural fairs) and to attract the Japanese corporate community into more active participation in the Uzbek economy have not yet yielded tangible outcomes. There are several reasons for such passive Japanese participation in Uzbekistan's economy when compared to Chinese and Korean participation. The first relates to the logistics of establishing and facilitating such cooperation. As mentioned in the section on the structure and implementation of roadmaps, Japanese interactions are coordinated by ROTOBO, which by its nature is not an organization with an executive branch. Thus, it has very limited capacity to perform any functions that can enforce decisions made within the intergovernmental economic cooperation committee. While ROTOBO's members regularly visit CA and organize various events, these only imitate productive activity without leading to any tangible outcomes. The reason ROTOBO is charged with the important mission of facilitating economic activity is related to the structure of the liberal market economy in Japan, where private interests are rarely connected to public institutions. Thus, ROTOBO considers its role to involve only facilitating interaction and not identifying or suggesting appropriate behaviors for the business community. While ROTOBO's approach is reasonable for Japan's conditions, such a structure for economic cooperation leaves CA countries, in particular, Uzbekistan and Kazakhstan, dissatisfied with their governmental institutions and ministries partnering with a nongovernmental organization such as ROTOBO. Many CA governments suggest that to revitalize relations in the practical realm, they must challenge ROTOBO's status and possibly replace it with a governmental institution capable of delivering tangible outcomes, as opposed to merely organizing forums and meetings.[62]

The second issue has to do with the behavioral pattern of the Japanese corporate community, which feels satiated with sufficient contracts and business opportunities generated in East Asia and elsewhere. For them, there is little incentive to penetrate CA markets, including Uzbekistan. Therefore, while Chinese businesses, which have governmental guarantees and support, find motivations to penetrate the geographically close CA states, Japanese companies do not yet see the added value in being offered an entrance to this region. To a large extent, the problems related to legal infrastructure and the perceived risks of this market significantly influence such decisions.

Figure 22. Japanese-Uzbek Cooperation in Economic Areas

No.	Planned Interaction	Aim	Essence
In trade and economic field			
1	Holding of the14th round of Joint Uzbek-Japan and Japan-Uzbek Economic Cooperation Committee sessions in Tokyo.	Deepening of economic cooperation and monitoring of current situation	14th round of Joint Uzbek-Japan and Japan-Uzbek Economic Cooperation Committee sessions in Tokyo planned for October 4, 2017
4	Facilitation of the participation of the Japanese companies in the Cotton Fair and the Agricultural Fair in Tashkent.	Concluding contracts for exports of cotton, textile and agricultural products to Japan	Facilitation of the participation of the Japanese companies in the Cotton Fair in Tashkent as well as the Agricultural Fair in Tashkent
11	Facilitation of mutual visits of corporate community of the two countries with presentations for cooperation potential.	Expansion of cooperation	- ROTOBO, May 25–26, 2017 - Hokkaido Intellect Tank, March–April, 2017 for preparing the concept of "Strengthening the potential of the agricultural sector of Uzbekistan" - Torishima company, M. Nishimura, rehabilitation of pump stations in Tashkent region

No.	Planned Interaction	Aim	Essence
12	Facilitation of participation of Japanese companies in privatization of property in Uzbekistan and introduction of Japanese technological innovations.	Sales of shares and properties	Offering participation in privatization (data-base of 150 companies has been formed and information on the possible objects of privatization has been channeled with the passports of the priva-tized buildings; work through the embassy on spreading the word on these properties continues)
13	Expanding coopera-tion in providing edu-cation to specialists in the fields of economy (grants for MA pro-grams through the channel of technical cooperation); prepara-tion of Global Public Leadership Program for public servants through JICA.	Education and training	15 scholarships for MA studies in 2017–2018; preparation of Global Public Leadership Program for public servants through JICA
14	Jupiter 2	Implementation of Jupiter 2 actions for 2017–2020.	Uzbekenergo and JICA

As a result, as indicated below, Japanese humanitarian assistance, government-provided educational grants and loans, and JICA-led assistance projects dominate the agenda for cooperation, thus attributing to Japan the role of one of the largest assistance providers but not of an economic partner.

Figure 23. JICA Disbursements to CA and the Caucasus

	Total Value of JICA programs (in millions of YEN)	Composition ratio %
Uzbekistan	38,898	73.8
Azerbaijan	5,055	9.6
Tajikistan	3,349	6.4
Kirgiz Republic	2,948	5.6
Georgia	1,803	3.4
Armenia	466	0.9
Kazakhstan	155	0.3
Turkmenistan	22	0

Source: JICA Activity Report, 2016, "East Asia and Central Asia: Toward Sustained Economic Development through Strengthening Regional Connectivity and Diversifying Industries," https://www.jica.go.jp/english/publications/reports/annual/2017/c8h0vm0000bws721-att/2017_06.pdf.

Conclusion

A few conclusions can be drawn from the outline of the economic cooperation roadmaps of China, Korea, and Japan. The first conclusion is that economic cooperation roadmaps merely represent the intentions of the governments and other nongovernmental organizations to pursue certain goals and objectives. In this sense, this paper treats these roadmaps as a type of political narrative. Thus, the mere fact that these roadmaps have been agreed upon does not necessarily imply that they will be implemented. However, they still represent very clearly formulated documents with actors, budgets, and time-frame definitions that can be treated as generating certain political messages.

Second, economic cooperation roadmaps are indicative of the approaches and goals of China, Japan,

Economic cooperation roadmaps are indicative of the approaches and goals of China, Japan, and Korea in Central Asia

and Korea in this part of the world. They indicate the expectations of cooperating with CA states, exemplified by the case of Uzbekistan. In particular, the Chinese approach indicated in the roadmap's agenda is to exploit China's competitive advantage of close geographical proximity to this energy-resource-endowed region. In addition, China aims to exploit its advantage in technological advances by exporting its machinery to Uzbekistan's for the country's further industrialization. In addition, China aims to use its abundant financial resources to fund certain projects that primarily benefit Chinese corporate interests while also having a certain positive impact on the Uzbek economy. Yet China emphasizes that its initiatives are to support Uzbekistan's developmental strategy for 2017–20; thus, for China, the Uzbek government's task is to ensure that the strategy's aims and goals are properly formulated to securely defend Uzbek interests. In this sense, it would be unrealistic to expect that China is in Uzbekistan to ensure that Uzbekistan benefits. In contrast, China aims to secure its own economic interests while leaving it to the Uzbek government to ensure that cooperation with China will benefit the Uzbek economy. In this sense, China-Uzbekistan cooperation is a pragmatic cooperation aimed to achieve each government's clearly defined goals. Very little emotional attachment is displayed by either government in pursuing these roadmaps.

Japanese roadmaps, on the contrary, lack the pragmatic goals and aims that clearly benefit the Japanese corporate community or the Japanese government. In contrast with the Chinese approach, Japanese roadmaps emphasize the Japanese commitment to developing Uzbekistan and strengthening its human capital development and capacity to deal with local economic problems. However, the largest problem in Japanese roadmaps is that they do not clearly demonstrate how the Japanese corporate community and taxpayers benefit from its engagement through their implementation.

Korean roadmaps represent the mode of engagement that combines the pragmatism seen in the Chinese roadmaps and the emotional attachment to developing Uzbekistan seen in the Japanese roadmaps. On the one hand, Korean roadmaps clearly aim to benefit the Korean business community, demonstrated by the number of projects and the spectrum of areas covered by those roadmaps. On the other hand, Korean roadmaps also include a huge cluster of human capital development, such as establishing a great number of educational institutions, supporting human resource development programs for Uzbek bureaucracy, supporting the increase of Uzbek nationals in the international organizations, providing know-how for establishing digital trade platforms, and providing know-how for entry into the World Trade Organization. These components of Korean roadmaps demonstrate Korea's message to Uzbekistan: it is interested in benefiting from the opportunities in the Uzbek economy, but it also aims to contribute to certain areas in which it has significant experience.

Third, these roadmaps are both a result and a consequence of the pattern of interactions between these states. While the frequency of interactions between the governments does not necessarily relate to the quality of those interactions, the cases of China, Korea, and Japan demonstrate that a certain relationship between the frequency and outcomes of the visits of heads of state and governments. As mentioned in the first section of this paper, the Chinese heads of state and governments are frequent visitors to Uzbekistan, sometimes visiting several times per year. In addition, leaders of the two countries meet at various events related to the SCO and BRI in China and elsewhere. Such frequency leads to denser discussions on various issues, thereby contributing to the increasing number of projects in economic cooperation roadmaps. This relationship has led to the inclusion of the largest number of projects in the roadmap of cooperation between China and Uzbekistan. Leaders of Korea and Uzbekistan do not meet as frequently as the leaders of China and Uzbekistan; they have met almost annually (in 1992, 1994, 1995, 1999, 2005, 2006, and twice in 2008, 2009, 2010, 2011, 2012, 2014, 2015, 2017), and their meetings happen annually or biannually depending on the agenda. Such frequency allows for constructive cooperation across various fields, resulting in less ambitious but still significant agendas for cooperation. While the total volume of contracts, in terms of amount, is not as high as those between China and Uzbekistan, the project spectrum exceeds that between China and Uzbekistan. At the same time, the leaders of Japan and Uzbekistan meet only occasionally, but once every several years. The leaders of Japan have visited CA and Uzbekistan only twice, and Uzbek leaders have visited Japan three times over the period of independence. While the level of high-official meetings is considerably high at the level of the Central

Asia plus Japan initiative, the process of preparing economic cooperation roadmaps intensifies before and at the time of visits of heads of
state. The agendas of the economic cooperation plans demonstrate
that the spectrum of the areas is rather limited and primarily focuses
on the interaction between the governments, leaving much potential
for further development.

The fourth observation relates to the areas covered by the economic cooperation roadmaps of the three states covered in this paper.
The Chinese economic cooperation roadmaps demonstrate the highest volume in terms of amounts of contracts and agreements. In terms
of areas of cooperation, they relate mainly to three areas: energy,
infrastructure development, and manufacturing. Korean roadmaps
do not match Chinese ones in terms of amounts; the spectrum of
projects and areas of cooperation exceed the Chinese-Uzbek economic cooperation roadmaps. Interestingly, the main actors within the
Korean-Uzbek economic cooperation maps consist of a large number
of smaller enterprises, while the
Chinese roadmaps are dominated
by larger enterprises working in
the fields of energy and infrastructure development. The share of
smaller enterprises in the Chinese-
Uzbek roadmaps is smaller when
compared to the Korean-Uzbek
roadmaps. This finding can be
explained by the difference in the
economic structures of China and
Korea as described in the section
of this paper dealing with the
issues of governance and economic cooperation. The Japanese-Uzbek
roadmaps are primarily dominated by the cooperation between the
governments and by framework agreements.

While Chinese-Uzbek economic cooperation roadmaps focus on economic cooperation, while Korean and the Japanese cooperation roadmaps focus on humanitarian cooperation

The fifth observation relates to the comparison of Chinese, Korean,
and Japanese roadmaps in the humanitarian field. While Chinese-
Uzbek economic cooperation roadmaps are focused on promotion
of economic cooperation, the share in the humanitarian field is very
limited. In contrast, Korean and the Japanese cooperation roadmaps include a large number of projects and initiatives related to

humanitarian cooperation. A significant number of projects initiated by Korea relate to the establishment of universities, research institutions, and research facilities. Similarly, the Japanese roadmaps relate to grants for educational activities and education-related projects of JICA. They might not necessarily relate to immediate income generation, but they contribute importantly to human capacity development in Uzbekistan, which advertently relates to the increase in economic potential.

The final observation relates to the spectrum of actors involved in the cooperation between the countries. In the Chinese case, the government plays the roles of both facilitator and executor of many agreements. In the Korean case, private corporate enterprises lead the way in fostering cooperation. Additionally, increased intensification of private economic activity in the country encourages the government to intensify its involvement. Japanese involvement demonstrates a different pattern in which public institutions of government and developmental assistance agencies lead the way in establishing cooperation. However, at this stage, such governmental activity does not necessarily translate into private enterprise involvement. This issue is somewhat improved in the 2018 economic roadmaps of Japan-Uzbek cooperation, which are not covered in this paper.

Endnotes

1. See, for example, Kirkham (2016) and Freeman (2018).
2. See, for example, Obydenkova (2011) and Alimov (2018).
3. See, for example, Yongquan (2018).
4. For the sake of simplicity, this paper uses "South Korea" and "Korea" interchangeably. In no part of this paper does "Korea" imply North Korea. For individual case studies, see Fumagalli (2016) and Dadabaev (2016).
5. See Dadabaev (2014a, 2018c).
6. See Dadabaev (2018d, 2018a).
7. See Dadabaev (2014b).
8. ibid.
9. For details, see Dadabaev (2013).
10. For details of the Japanese discursive strategy in CA in comparative perspective see Dadabaev (Forthcoming 2019.
11. Presentation, Ministry of Foreign Affairs of Japan, accessed September 25, 2018, https://www.mofa.go.jp/files/000117998.pdf.
12. For details of the Indo-Pacific Strategy see Ministry of Foreign Affairs of Japan, "Priority Policy for Development Cooperation 2017," https://www.mofa.go.jp/files/000259285.pdf.
13. See Dadabaev (Forthcoming).
14. For details see "Number of foreign residents in Korea more than doubles in decade", The Korea Herald, June 21, 2017, accessed on August 24, 2018, at http://www.koreaherald.com/view.php?ud=20170621000598.
15. For details, see Dadabaev (2018f.)
16. For example, see "Decree of the President of Uzbekistan on Reconfirming 'Agreement between Republic of Uzbekistan and People's Republic of China on Facilitating Smooth International Road Transportation'," http://nrm.uz/contentf?doc=508717_postanovlenie_prezidenta_respubliki_uzbekistan_ot_20_07_2017_g_n_pp-3143_ob_utverjdenii_mejdunarodnogo_dogovora&products=1_vse_zakonodatelstvo_uzbekistana.
17. For examples of this, see Dadabaev (2018).
18. For details, see Dadabaev (2018e).

19. Uzbekistan's Development Strategy 2017–2021, accessed September 25, 2018, http://old.lex.uz/pages/getpage.aspx?lact_id=3107042.

20. For instance, Uzbek Foreign Trade and the PRC Ministry of Commerce signed memoranda to facilitate the organization of producer exhibitions in May 2017.

21. For instance, in a private conversation in September 2017 in Tashkent, a Japanese embassy official described such an Uzbek-Japanese cooperation structure as impossible due to a regulatory function of the Japanese government, which prevents it from forcing Japanese corporations into foreign cooperation schemes.

22. See "Agreement between Governments of the Republic of Uzbekistan and the People's Republic of China on Creation of Uzbek-Chinese Intergovernmental Committee for Cooperation, Beijing," http://www.lex.uz/pages/GetAct. aspx?lact_id=1986611.

23. ibid. See the appendices to the agreement.

24. See http://www.jahonnews.uz/en/ekonomika/316/36956/.

25. Decree of the President of Uzbekistan, accessed September 23, 2017, http://www.norma.uz/raznoe/postanovlenie_prezidenta_respubliki_uzbekistan_ot_27_09_2017_g_pp-3293.

26. "Shanghai spirit" refers to a norm that connects the issues for cooperation prioritized by both countries without seeking unilateral gains. This norm also implies the importance of mutual sacrifices and compromises for mutual gain.

27. Ministry of Economy of Uzbekistan, accessed September 23, 2017, https://mineconomy.uz/ru/node/1091.

28. This amount includes both Chinese and Uzbek shares in the deals signed. Thus, the pure Chinese contribution/investment in the deals is roughly US$10 billion; the rest accounts for Uzbekistan's contributions, including monetary contributions as well as the costs of land and infrastructure development.

29. MOFA of Japan, https://www.mofa.go.jp/mofaj/press/release/press4_001142.html.

30. MOFA of Japan, https://www.mofa.go.jp/mofaj/files/000047885.pdf.

31. Decree of the President of Uzbekistan (in Russian), http://nrm.uz/contentf?doc=508717_postanovlenie_prezidenta_respubliki_uzbekistan_ot_20_07_2017_g_n_pp-3143_ob_utverjdenii_mejdunarodnogo_dogovora&products=1_vse_zakonodatelstvo_uzbekistana.

32. For details, see https://kloop.kg/blog/2017/09/09/uzbekistan-hochet-postroit-trassu-andizhan-osh-irkeshtam-kashgar/.

33. See, for example, https://www.rferl.org/a/qishloq-ovozi-kyrgyzstan-uzbekistan-china-railway/28713485.html.

34. See http://www.tashkenttimes.uz/economy/930-china-to-help-build-second-tunnel-at-kamchik-pass.

35. See http://interfax.az/view/705802 and https://news.tj/ru/news/tajikistan/economic/20170615/uzbekistan-nameren-narastit-postavki-gaza-v-kitai.

36. See http://www.tashkenttimes.uz/economy/1016-uzbekistan-china-jv-new-silk-road-oil-and-gas-commences-drilling-in-bukhara.

37. ibid.

38. For details, see Voloshin, George. 2017. "Central Asia Ready to Follow China's Lead Despite Russian Ties," Eurasia Daily Monitor 14 (71). Accessed September 23, 2017, https://jamestown.org/program/central-asia-ready-

follow-chinas-lead-despite-russian-ties/. See also http https://eurasianet.org/s/uzbekistan-presidents-china-trip-yields-giant-rewards.

39. See http://www.review.uz/novosti-main/item/11217-uzbekistan-i-kitaj-pod-pisali-soglashenij-na-summu-bolee-20-mlrd.
40. ibid.
41. See https://www.gazeta.uz/ru/2017/09/07/coal/.
42. See http://www.tashkenttimes.uz/economy/1060-program-for-increased-use-of-biogas-in-farms-adopted-in-uzbekistan.
43. See http://mswrecyclingplant.com/beston-municipal-solid-waste-plant-uzbekistan/.
44. For details, see http://news.uzreport.uz/news_4_e_153308.html.
45. See https://uzdaily.com/PYLnM/articles-id-40176.htm.
46. See https://www.uzdaily.com/articles-id-37934.htm.
47. See https://www.gazeta.uz/ru/2017/09/29/lifts/.
48. See "O merakh po organizatsii sovremennogo proizvodstva detskih prinadlezh-nostei i igrushek v gorode Tashkente" [Decree of the President of the Republic of Uzbekistan on measures for organization of production of children's acces-sories and toys in the city of Tashkent], July 6, 2017.
49. See https://www.gazeta.uz/ru/2017/08/02/toys/.
50. For details, see https://www.gazeta.uz/ru/2017/09/13/cluster/>.
51. See https://www.uzdaily.com/articles-id-39970.htm.
52. See http://ut.uz/en/business/fez-angren-may-become-the-largest-producer-of-porcelain-in-the-country/.
53. See http://china-uz-friendship.com/?p=12945>.
54. See https://uzreport.news/economy/v-uzbekistane-budet-sozdano-sp-po-proiz-vodstvu-bumajnoy-produktsii.
55. See http://www.jinshengroup.com/en/stations/532661b60b/index.php/5327ed9b0a?id=161.
56. ibid.
57. See http://ru.sputniknews-uz.com/economy/20170811/6014975/kitai-sez-djizak-proekti.html.
58. MOFA of Korea, International Economic Affairs Bureau, International Eco-nomic Cooperation Division, http://english.moef.go.kr/pc/selectTbPressCenter-Dtl.do?boardCd=N0001&seq=4440.
59. Government Development Center of Uzbekistan, https://www.egovernment.uz/en/press_center/news/meeting-with-the-delegation-of-the-company-ktnet/.
60. See https://www.uzdaily.com/articles-id-41716.htm.
61. See https://www.uzdaily.com/articles-id-41705.htm.
62. This has been indicated to the author on many occasions, both during the in-terviews at the CA missions in Tokyo and by governmental officials. The most recent occasion was an off-the-record interview with a high ranking official in one of the Embassies of CA states in Tokyo on July 2, 2018.

Bibliography

Alimov, Rashid. 2018. "The Shanghai Cooperation Organisation: Its Role and Place in the Development of Eurasia," Journal of Eurasian Studies 9 (2):114–124.

Dadabaev, Timur. 2013. "Japan's Search for Its Central Asian Policy: Between Idealism and Pragmatism," Asian Survey 53 (3):506–532.

———. 2014a. "Chinese and Japanese Foreign Policies toward Central Asia from a Comparative Perspective," Pacific Review 27 (1):123–145.

———. 2014b."Shanghai Cooperation Organization (SCO) Regional Identity Formation from the Perspective of the Central Asian States," Journal of Contemporary China 23 (85):102-118.

———. 2016. "Japan's ODA Assistance Scheme and Central Asian Engagement," Journal of Eurasian Studies 7 (1):24–38.

———. 2018a. "Engagement and Contestation: The Entangled Imagery of the Silk Road," Cambridge Journal of Eurasian Studies 2 (2018). doi: 10.22261/ CJES.Q4GIV6.

———. 2018b. "Japan Attempts to Crack the Central Asian Frontier," AsiaGlobal Online, August 30. https://www.asiaglobalonline.hku.hk/japan-central-asia-uzbekistan-kazakhstan/.

———. 2018c. "Japanese and Chinese Infrastructure Development Strategies in Central Asia," Japanese Journal of Political Science 19 (3):1–20. doi: 10.1017/S1468109918000178.

———. 2018d. "'Silk Road'" as Foreign Policy Discourse: The Construction of Chinese, Japanese and Korean Engagement Strategies in Central Asia," Journal of Eurasian Studies 9 (2018): 30–41. doi:10.1016/j.euras.2017.12.003.

———. 2018e. "The Chinese Economic Pivot in Central Asia and Its Implications for Post-Karimov Re-emergence of Uzbekistan," Asian Survey 58 (4):747–769.

———. 2018f. "Uzbekistan as Central Asian Game Changer? Uzbekistan's Foreign Policy Construction in the Post-Karimov Era," Asian Journal of Comparative Politics (2018):1–14.

———. Forthcoming 2019. "Discourses of Rivalry or Rivalry of Discourses: Discursive Strategies of China and Japan in Central Asia," The Pacific Review.

———. Forthcoming. "Revisiting Japan's Silk Road Master Narratives," Asia Pacific Issues.

Freeman, Carla P. 2018. "New strategies for an old rivalry? China–Russia Relations in Central Asia after the Energy Boom," Pacific Review. doi: 10.1080/09512748.2017.1398775.

Fumagalli, Matteo. 2016. "Growing Inter-Asian Connections: Links, Rivalries, and Challenges in South Korean–Central Asian Relations," Journal of Eurasian Studies 7 (1): 39–48.

Ksenia Kirkham. 2016. "The Formation of the Eurasian Economic Union: How Successful Is the Russian Regional Hegemony?" Journal of Eurasian Studies 7 (2): 111–128.

Lain, Sarah. 2017. "Russia and China: Cooperation and Competition in Central Asia." In Chinese Foreign Policy under Xi, edited by Tiang Boon Hoo, 74–95. London: Routledge.

Li, Yongquan. 2018. "The Greater Eurasian Partnership and the Belt and Road Initiative: Can the Two Be Linked?" Journal of Eurasian Studies 9 (2):94–99.

Obydenkova, Anastassia. 2011. "Comparative Regionalism: Eurasian Cooperation and European Integration: The Case for Neofunctionalism?" Journal of Eurasian Studies 2 (2):87–102.

Voloshin, George. 2017. "Central Asia Ready to Follow China's Lead Despite Russian Ties," Eurasia Daily Monitor 14 (71). Accessed September 23, 2017, https://jamestown.org/program/central-asia-ready-follow-chinas-lead-despite-russian-ties/.

Acknowledgments

This work was supported by JSPS KAKENHI Grants Number JP15KK0108 (Fostering Joint International Research) and JP16K03523. The research for this study was supported by an East-West Center Asia Studies Fellowship. I would like to thank the staff at the East-West Center in Washington office for their encouragement and support.

www.ingramcontent.com/pod-product-compliance
Lightning Source LLC
Chambersburg PA
CBHW060647210326
41520CB00010B/1767